Praise for *Marginlands*

'*Marginlands* is a tour de force, a magnificent first book about India's marginalized landscapes and inhabitants (human and more-than-human), which takes its readers from the high Himalayas to the Sundarban delta, from the deserts of the Thar to the climate-change-ravaged Keralan coastline and beyond. Born of hard, committed, long-term first-hand witnessing of places and people, it is written with compassion, compressed elegance of observation, and urgent political force. Kumar-Rao's book joins new voices, including Yuvan Aves (*Intertidal*) and Neha Sinha (*Wild and Wilful*), proving that a powerful, hopeful resurgence of Indian nature writing is happening right now'
Robert Macfarlane, author of *Mountains of the Mind* and *Underland*

'Arati Kumar-Rao writes with grace and empathy about traditional forms of resilience and how they help ordinary people survive, and even flourish, in the most demanding environments – and about the often devastating impacts of clumsy interventions by the state. This is some of the best environmental writing I have read in a long time'
Amitav Ghosh, author of *The Hungry Tide* and *Gun Island*

'From startling images and evocative prose to brilliant sketches, what a glittering array of tools Arati Kumar-Rao has in her quiver! She is going to make a lot of people exceedingly envious'
Pradip Krishen, naturalist, filmmaker and author of *Trees of Delhi*

'Our grandchildren will be reading Arati Kumar-Rao to understand the momentous decisions that our generation faced – and, shamefully, more often than not shirked – in valuing and safeguarding the last dazzling but imperilled ecological riches of the Indian subcontinent. Luminously written with slashing honesty and profound empathy, Kumar-Rao gifts us with a traveller's haunting account of the vast stakes involved in India's environmental emergencies, as well as moving homages to the keepers of traditional systems of knowledge who, if we only listened to them as carefully as she does, could help rescue what remains'
Paul Salopek, two-time Pulitzer Prize-winning journalist and writer

'Arati Kumar-Rao has written a book from the heart, infused with her poetic voice and humanistic soul, on topics she has explored for many years. Drawing on her multiple talents of writing, photography and sketching, Kumar-Rao has documented pressing issues affecting India while making much deeper connections with the relationship of humans to their resources, lands, and the wildlife they must coexist with. A monumental lesson for all of humanity to pay attention to so that we might redirect our course to a better, more sustainable future, this book is a work for the ages'
Ed Kashi, photojournalist, filmmaker and educator

'Arati Kumar Rao's timely book comes as a warning in a world that's riddled with too many difficulties. Richly intense writing ... A marvellous treatise on life on the margins, on cultures on the brink and on the disappearance awaiting ecosystems. It is a lesson and, at the same time, a heartfelt tribute to India's diverse ecology. *Marginlands* is a work that makes you despair as well as hope'
Rahul Singh, *Deccan Herald*

'In chapter after chapter, [Kumar-Rao] tells poignant stories of loss, including those that can't be quantified ... Through her meticulous research and impassioned storytelling, she unveils the multifaceted challenges faced by local communities, wildlife and ecosystems on the brink of irrevocable change. [Her] eloquent prose breathes life into the pages ... the fragility of these regions becomes palpable, igniting a sense of urgency to protect what remains. [*Marginlands*] is yet another reminder that the fate of our environment is intricately braided with our own'
Nawaid Anjum, *Federal*

'A few pages into the book, I realized that if Kumar-Rao's pictures are a brush-stroke, words are definitely her sword. She writes with searing clarity, weaving strands of history, prose, and science together into a compelling narrative. *Marginlands* does not weep; it shares the wisdom of ancient people and mixes their native language into the main story ... and in doing so, offers us a front-seat view of the subtle yet tectonic

changes taking place in ecosystems across the country ... I would urge you to read this book. This is bold writing'
Bahar Dutt, *Frontline*

'Captures the tumultuous lives – both human and non-human – of those who inhabit the margins of the subcontinent'
Divya Gandhi, *Hindu*

'One of [the] finest chroniclers of [our] land'
Sonya Dutta Choudhury, *Hindustan Times*

'Kumar-Rao maps expansively, and probes intensively, a precisely balanced and highly fragile ecosystem and the people who have lived with it'
Latha Anantharaman, *India Today*

'Arati Kumar-Rao uses the skills in her toolbox to document the country's vulnerable landscapes, ecosystems and populations'
Sucheta Chakraborty, *Mid-day*

'These are stories that remind us of what we could save if we listened to the world around us a bit more … One of the most active voices in the environmental storytelling space in India, in *Marginlands* Kumar-Rao goes deeper to understand these marginalized landscapes through the people who live there'
Nitin Sreedhar, *Mint Lounge*

'Timely … Arati Kumar-Rao documents first-hand accounts of apathy toward the environment and how it is affecting lives on the fringes of our country'
Shail Desai, *Moneycontrol*

Thought-provoking … *Marginlands* is among the most timely non-fictions to have released [in 2023]'
Mayank Jain Parichha, *New Indian Express*

'Exemplary ... Kumar-Rao evocatively tells us the stories of the wasted landscapes of our country and of the unforgivable official neglect of traditional wisdom and knowledge systems, which sustained the people living here .... The writing is riveting ... This book needs to be mandatory reading for all the planning mandarins who ought to get out of their offices and do the kind of fieldwork Kumar-Rao has done, before launching their grandiose projects'
Ranjit Lal, *Open*

'Kumar-Rao's commitment to spotlighting the stories of people affected by decisions taken far away from their reality is reflected in her words, images and illustrations ... The book has the lucidity of fiction and the factual punches of non-fiction ... It's like she has created a time capsule, documenting practices that have been handed down over generations, which help people live in harmony with the land, or of people who have lost and lived with the vagaries of nature and human decisions. For anyone concerned with the environment, the lives of people, and the often convoluted business of coexistence in times of polycrisis, the book is a must-read'
Shatakshi Gawade, *Sanctuary Asia*

'[Arati Kumar-Rao] manages to tell human-centric stories … and captures what's at the centre of any argument that's made to save nature: that humans' very existence relies on its preservation'
Saurabh Sharma, *Scroll.in*

'There are very few storytellers who can let go of their comforts and immerse themselves in the harsh environments they talk about. Arati Kumar-Rao is one of them, which is why her work never fails to inform and astound … What makes this book special is that it's not an academic exercise on Indian landscapes. It is more about the lives, both human and wild, that are an intrinsic part of these ecosystems. Rao combines folklore, science, history, personal accounts and policy decisions to paint images through words that illuminate our understanding. It's a book that lays bare the ecological wonders and human blunders of India'
Manu Moudgil, *Tribune*

marginlands

marginlands

INDIAN LANDSCAPES ON THE BRINK

ARATI KUMAR-RAO

PICADOR INDIA

First published in India 2023 by Picador India
First published in paperback 2024 by Picador India
an imprint of Pan Macmillan Publishing India Private Limited
707 Kailash Building
26 K. G. Marg, New Delhi 110001
www.panmacmillan.co.in

Pan Macmillan, The Smithson, 6 Briset Street, Farringdon, London EC1M 5NR
Associated companies throughout the world
www.panmacmillan.com

ISBN 978-81-19300-33-4

This book was supported by a grant from Rohini Nilekani Philanthropies.

'In the Shifting Embrace of the Ganga' and 'Into the Hidden Land' were first published in *Emergence Magazine* in May 2023 and March 2021 respectively.

A version of 'Listening to Landscapes' was first published as part of the 'Out of Eden Walk' series in NationalGeographic.org.

3 5 7 9 8 6 4 2

Typeset in Adobe Garamond Pro by R. Ajith Kumar, New Delhi
Printed and bound in India by Thomson Press India Ltd.

FSC www.fsc.org MIX Paper | Supporting responsible forestry FSC® C010615

To my parents,
from whom I have learned so much

CONTENTS

I don't try to fool myself that the stories of individuals are themselves arguments. I just believe that better arguments, maybe even better policies, get formulated when we know more about ordinary lives.

KATHERINE BOO,
Behind the Beautiful Forevers[1]

PROLOGUE
Gathering String

It may be that when we no longer know what to do we have come to our real work, and that when we no longer know which way to go we have begun our real journey.

WENDELL BERRY,
Standing by Words[1]

Bangalore
July 2007

OUTSIDE, THE RAIN HAMMERED DOWN, RELENTLESS IN ITS intensity. I huddled under the covers, in the grip of a fever that refused to let up.

At 2:30 that afternoon, with a thermometer read-out of 104°F, I logged into a call to China, cued up my presentation and passed the next hour in a febrile stupor. Shivering and exhausted, I dragged myself out of my den and up a flight of stairs, swallowed a paracetamol and crashed into oblivion.

When I woke up, it was night, and my temperature had kicked up another notch – to 105°F.

Several days of blood tests and hospital visits later, I learned that I had paratyphoid. I am allergic to antibiotics; my recovery was going to be slow and precarious. I took leave from the multinational corporation where I worked as a market researcher, studying technology consumption behaviour in the Asia-Pacific region and its implications for marketing strategy.

Days passed in a delirium. The monsoon kept up a tympanic backbeat to my misery, crashing against the windowpanes. My mother installed herself as resident caregiver, disciplinarian and guardian angel; she fed me nutritious meals and maintained vigil to ensure I did nothing in the way of work. Huddled under blankets, I drifted in and out of fever dreams.

My childhood in eighties' Bombay was a mix of many worlds. My father worked for a company that housed its employees in a gated colony – a wooded, hilly township accessible by a kilometre-long road that led away from the metropolis. My second-floor bedroom window was curtained by the boughs of trees on which sang orioles and ioras, barbets and bee-eaters, bulbuls and parakeets.

I was seven when a spotted owlet hopped onto our balcony late one evening, and I remember my pre-teen self feeling an unprecedented exhilaration. I spent my teenage evenings walking through brush and cycling on paths that rose and fell at steep inclines; I devoured books in the shade of a mango tree; friends plucked gooseberries that I carried in the swell of my skirt to someone's porch, where we sucked on them with lips that puckered against the tartness – a life that was a part of, and yet apart from, the press of humanity that is Bombay.

My father, an engineer by training, worked for a thermal power company. Though a trained nutritionist, my mother taught English, science and geography at a local school. Papa did not believe in owning a car, and we lived in a city where public transport – Bombay's BEST buses and suburban trains – satisfied all of our travel needs. He role-modelled cycling to the closest highway and then using a bus to reach the nearest train station that took him to the other end of town for work. Every day, Mamma walked to and back from school, a mile from where we lived. Thus, my sister and I grew up walking, cycling, riding buses and trains all over our island megacity.

Even though my father's scope of work did not involve renewable energy sources, he was convinced about their efficacy as far back as the early eighties – long before climate change and clean, green energy became catchphrases. When I was eight, he built a solar cooker for our home – a wooden box painted black on the outside and lined with aluminium foil on the inside, with four reflective flaps that directed sunlight into the cavity. We cooked rice in it, and sometimes lentils – a tad unsatisfactorily, according to Mamma. It fell upon my sister and me to take turns running up to the terrace to orient the cooker towards the sun every few hours.

My family's reading tastes were eclectic: my father introduced us to literature as diverse as Kalidasa, Shakespeare, Mahatma Gandhi, Masanobu Fukuoka and Wendell Berry. Mamma, who comes from a family of academics, insisted on instilling communication skills in us. Good writing – including handwriting – and public speaking were important parts of my school life. On Sundays Papa would take us birdwatching. My sister and I would wake up at 4:30 a.m., as would some of the neighbourhood kids. Papa took us all in tow, the party walking a kilometre to the main road to catch one BEST bus, then another, until we reached Sanjay Gandhi National Park by daybreak. Here we would trek several kilometres through thick forests and across streams, binoculars around our necks, eager eyes straining to find birds and any other wildlife that might have been dwelling in those parts.

Those were exhilarating times. I devoured Salim Ali's *Book of Indian Birds*,[2] memorizing bird calls, what they ate, how long they lived, poring over the illustrations, planning 'expeditions' through the neighbouring woods with my sister for company.

In those days, a Wendell Berry poem that my father read to us seeped deep into my teenage mind. 'Reverdure'[3] began with an ode to curiosity …

You never know
What you are going to learn

… and went on to alternate between turning inwards and peeking outwards at the land, expounding an ethic that was gentle and harmonious, enduring and renewing – one that would serve as a lodestar for me decades later.

No leaf falls there that is lost;
all that falls rises, opens,
sings; what was, is.

We lived in a small apartment, 1,100 square feet – two bedrooms, a living room, a kitchen and a tiny room in the back that my parents, both voracious readers, had converted into a library. It was my refuge when guests came over; I would tune out the sound of conversations and tune into the world of words.

But one conversation refused to be shut out. My grand-uncle, a senior economist with the World Bank, visited us every other year from the United States. While my mother and my grand-aunt went into their private huddle to bring each other up to date on family news, I sat hunched behind a pale blue cotton curtain, my antennae tuned to the male voices in the living room – voices that started out low and cordial but tensed and grew in volume and vigour within minutes.

In the eighties, massive hydropower dams were still being built all over the world under the auspices of the World Bank. My father, who marched with protesters carrying 'Save The Western

Ghats' banners, and with activists who advocated for protecting Kerala's Silent Valley (he would later join the Narmada Bachao Andolan too), was dead set against large dams, believing them to carry an enormous ecological and social cost.

Long before world opinion began to look askance at those 'temples of modern India', my father had understood the price we would pay for every such interruption of a living, flowing, inhabited river. My grand-uncle took the opposite tack, pushing the merits of big hydro. As the evening wore on, their exchanges intensified and their faces reddened with the vehemence of their contrasting positions, until they ran out of breath as well as arguments and agreed to disagree.

My father, back then, was in a minority of one in his opposition to unplanned, unbridled development. It made a mark on me – his courage to stand for his convictions. My grand-uncle and other relatives, who came home and got caught up in these debates, were highly educated, erudite men, some of them tenured professors in American universities. How was it that none of them could see what my father recognized so early on?

That led me to wonder how, since arguments were clearly ineffective, one could fruitfully communicate fundamental ecological issues to the public; tell stories that married hydrology, ecology, social science and lucid communication; and reach past rhetoric to open minds to the unfamiliar and the inconvenient.

Those preoccupations stayed with me through my years in India as a master's student of physics, and later as a graduate student of design and business administration in Phoenix, Arizona, and remained a constant as I went to work, rushing from one meeting to the next in the conference rooms of a multinational corporation, first in the US and then in Bangalore.

That July night, as I lay on sheets drenched with the sweat of my agitations, all those lived experiences washed over me with renewed energy. It was as if that enforced pause from the frenetic pace of corporate life was exactly what I needed for clarity. Tossing about on my sickbed, I asked myself over and over: 'When will you stop doing what you *can* do and start doing what you really *want* to do?'

A line I had read and absorbed at some point came back to me, as if in answer to my question: 'And the day came when the risk to remain tight in a bud was more painful than the risk it took to blossom.'

In time, I recovered. Soon after my convalescence, on a decisive day in September 2007, I composed one of the hardest emails I have ever written to one of the best bosses I've ever had. I told her I wanted to quit my well-paying corporate job and venture into the uncertain world of environmental storytelling. 'I want to read, research, shoot and write about the fate of our landscapes,' I wrote.

Having cut the cord that bound me to my day job and decided to become a storyteller, I realized I had no idea how to go about it. I knew no one in Bangalore – editors, writers, or anyone who may have been interested in the kind of work I envisaged doing. I cold-called magazines, wrote emails to strangers, submitted story pitches and even fully composed stories, not knowing if I'd ever hear back.

I even got published in a few travel magazines – it wasn't what I had set out to do, and the few articles that did get published didn't fetch much income either. To make ends meet, I consulted with a market research firm and freelanced for my previous corporate employer. I bought a full-frame digital SLR camera and some cutting-edge lenses, blowing through what was left of my savings. Travelling and exploring geographies, I spent far more than I was making. I logged on to Facebook and Twitter to connect with journalists, editors, wildlife biologists, hydrologists and environmental activists. Many were generous with their time, guiding and teaching me, pointing me to resources, correcting misconceptions, taking me along on field trips.

Five years after my exit from corporate life – five years of learning, watching, doing – I realized that if I wanted to pursue my passion in earnest, I would need to give it my all; there could be no half measures. So I stopped consulting, giving up my safety net in order to fully commit to storytelling.

It was in 2012 that Twitter led me to Prem Panicker, managing editor of Yahoo! India at the time. At a meeting in a coffee shop with a different acquaintance I knew from social media, I had learnt about an ancient method of rainwater harvesting in the deep Thar. I wanted to pursue that story, I told Prem. He said that Yahoo would give me space to tell my story, even if they could not pay for travel.

But I was determined. Dipping into my savings, I booked tickets and set off for Rajasthan, flying from Bangalore to Jodhpur, where I met with Pradip Krishen, who was restoring desert ecosystems around Mehrangarh Fort. Together, with his team of naturalists – Harsha and Payal – we drove into the deep Thar beyond Jaisalmer, to explore. A few days later, I broke away from the team and went off to pursue the story I'd come for. All I had with me was the name and number of a shepherd-farmer in Ramgarh, a border-outpost town an hour or two northwest of the golden city of Jaisalmer. I got to the Jaisalmer bus stop and, weighted down by my backpack and camera bag, clambered onto a crowded bus which dropped me off a few hours later at a crossroads tea stall.

There was no sign of Chhattar Singh, the shepherd-farmer, and no response to my calls. I settled down at the tea stall and ordered my second cup. He materialized presently. A slight man of about fifty years with a head full of hair, dressed in a white kurta-pyjama, climbed out of an autorickshaw. 'Namaskaar,' he said with hands folded and a smile that revealed bright white teeth. Hauling my bags into the three-wheeler, we climbed in and went a short distance to the small stone house where I was to stay. There were two bare rooms – one locked, one open. Chhattar Singh motioned for me to take the open room. There was no bed; only a dhurrie on the floor, a fan, and a single naked bulb dangling from the ceiling.

I stepped out onto the porch to find two plastic chairs and a plastic table on which rested a plastic can of water. We sat down, and I began to ask him about the area. He interrupted me before I could make much headway. 'How much time do you have?'

I had only booked a one-way ticket, I told him, as I had no idea how long I would need in the desert. He smiled. Somehow I had offered the right answer; Chhattar Singh would not be hurried.

Over the next few days I walked the desert with Chhattar Singh in the blazing heat of summer. I saw what he showed me, listened to his stories, took notes as he explained how villagers in the area prepared the desert floor to harvest rainwater. And I learned a lesson that would set the tone for how I would tell my own stories: to really understand a landscape, you have to invest time, live in it, become one with it. 'You can't tell this story,' Chhattar Singh had said to me on the porch on my first day in his village, 'if you don't see for yourself how the desert changes with the seasons and how my people adapt to it.'

I called Prem and told him I would need an entire year for this one story alone. At first there was silence, as Prem was likely considering his options. But I knew the man was committed to The Story, among the last of his tribe. *Whatever it takes to tell it in the best possible way* has always been his mantra. 'Do what you have to do,' he said.

Starting in 2013, I returned to Ramgarh almost every month, observing the desert, living amidst its people, walking with shepherds as they tended their flocks, watching the landscape change, drinking endless cups of chai and engaging in *bantal*, the word the locals use for aimless conversations.

But 'aimless' can be relative. A reporter on assignment engages in transactional conversations, armed with a list of questions she wants answered; there is no time or inclination for digressions. But digressions can lead you down interesting avenues, as I discovered when a casual sentence heard over a fourth cup of chai spawned an idea for a story – it would have scarcely occurred to me in one hurried, agenda-driven visit.

I paid for those trips to the desert out of my own pocket, decimating my savings further. But in return, the time spent there instilled in me a deep respect for the landscape that far outweighed the costs. There was no substitute for giving time, paying attention and closely observing the land and the intricately interconnected relationships that played out on it. No substitute either for 'seeing' with all your senses. Had I not experienced the desert through the seasons, had I been content with one stint in the desert – or two – I would not have begun to fathom the land's rhythm which informs every aspect of lives lived against all odds.

Around this time, I came across a map of India's northeast with tiny black bars all over it – each bar a dam. The government planned to dam all the tributaries of the mighty Brahmaputra river, some of them several times over. What this would do to the fragile ecology of the Eastern Himalaya was beyond imagining – I felt I had to document that large river basin in its current state, and follow its fate over the years as the government's plans fructified.

Thus, in 2014, I turned my focus to the Ganga–Brahmaputra–Meghna basin, the most populated river basin in the world, where large hydropower dams and barrages had already played havoc with lives and landscapes.

I couldn't have sent Yahoo a vaguer pitch: 'I want to go to the basin, walk around and tell stories.' *What stories exactly?* 'I wouldn't know until I get there.' *How long a trip and how many stories?* 'I can't say.' Stories of the land take as long as they take; they can hardly adhere to a schedule or abide by an editor's clock. Yet, miraculously, my editor at Yahoo flashed the green light, and I set off in pursuit.

Following a thread I had picked up in Upper Assam, I went to Arunachal Pradesh, climbing back down to Lower Assam to pursue a related thread. It led me across the border into Bangladesh, where I found several other pieces of string. Thus was born 'River Diaries', a project that allowed me to criss-cross the Ganga–Brahmaputra–Meghna basin, telling stories as I went. This lasted for six months, until the Yahoo management changed, corporate priorities took over, and the funding dried up.

By then, however, I was fully vested in telling these stories and telling them my way. So I secured loans, applied for grants, and kept travelling, documenting landscapes, connecting dots. Sometimes I would not publish for months if I felt I didn't understand enough or I had not seen seasonal change that was central to the story.

Rainer Maria Rilke likens the life of an artist to that of a tree, and his words are true of storytelling about landscapes too: 'In this there is no measuring with time, a year doesn't matter, and ten years are nothing.'[4] That need to absorb myself in landscapes deepened further with time and was reaffirmed when I came upon a wise professor's urgings. Environmental stories, Rob Nixon writes in 'Slow Violence and the Environmentalism of the Poor', are about 'slow violence'[5] – a kind of destruction that unleashes itself incrementally, over seasons, often over generations. Unspectacular and sometimes imperceptible, it can be spatially dispersed: a disruption in one place can affect landscapes and lives several hundreds of miles away. Those who live in these landscapes – and the ecosystems themselves – die by a thousand cuts.

In my work, I was seeing several examples first-hand. The fifty-year-old barrage at Farakka, the head of the Ganga delta in West Bengal, that is wreaking havoc to this day is a veritable instance of 'slow violence' – and it is hardly the only one.

Almost every account in this book, therefore, is an example of misguided decisions, warnings wilfully ignored, evidence disregarded, inevitably paving the way for impending or currently unravelling disasters that may never make the news.

This book is not meant to be a comprehensive account of India's landscapes – far from it. It is rather a record of my early attempts at gathering string from all over, of returning to places to pick up old threads and find new ones, of knotting them together to weave a fabric that might, eventually, come together in a tapestry that celebrates a more gentle, just and equitable land ethic. For it is my belief that the ancient practice of listening to the land and doing right by it can yet be reclaimed.

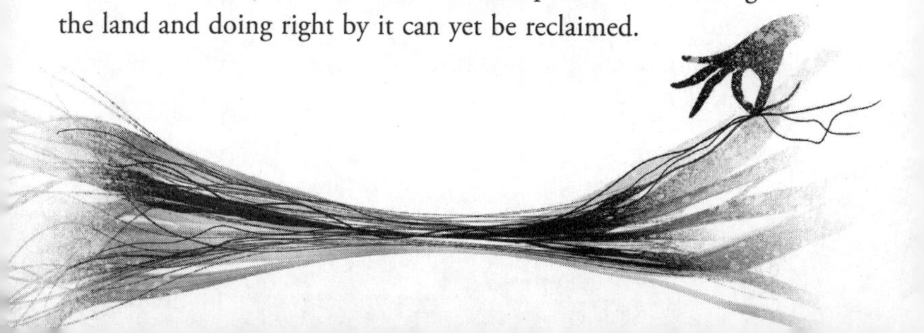

PART 1
THE DESERT

A LIQUID MEMORY

The Kurukshetra war having ended, Krishna and Arjuna were returning to Dwarka through a vast stretch of desert. On Mount Trikut, the rishi Uttung was practising austerities. Krishna bowed to him and, pleased with his devotion, offered him a boon. The rishi, who scarcely spared a thought for himself, said: 'If I have any merit, my Lord, may this region never suffer from scarcity of water.'

'Let it be so,' said Krishna.

Anupam Mishra,
(adapted from) *The Radiant Raindrops of Rajasthan*[1]

THE SOFT SAND RIPPLES IN THE BREEZE, GATHERING OVER TIME into giant arcuate waves. The dunes run lengthwise for tens of kilometres, riding the winds that blow northeast to southeast and back again. Shaped by the winds, they swell and rise and fall away into valleys of green – kair trees with their caper-like fruit, grasses, spindly desert plants – and then rise again. This is the brousse tigrée, the alternating pattern of golden sand and green valleys that, seen from above, gives the desert the appearance of a tiger's stripes.

There is no elegant way to climb a dune. The sand is pliant and giving; when you step onto the slope your foot sinks. As you pull your foot out, your weight shifts, and now the other foot sinks. With each step, the sand rolls down around you until you feel as if you're falling backwards. It's a sand-bog treadmill. The trick, I learned through trial and frustrating error, is to slouch forward and slog along until eventually reaching the top.

These dunes, just a few kilometres from India's western border with Pakistan, are higher and longer than those in Sam, which is to the south and pocked over with camel hoofprints, colonized by tented camps – a tourist magnet. Here there are no visitors; only the occasional shepherd with his flock, or a lone trader looking to buy desert goats and sheep.

Chhattar Singh sits cross-legged atop one of the highest dunes, his quietude untouched by the wild wind. As the sun travels overhead, he begins to dig. Sticking his hand into the dune, he pulls out a lump of darker, coffee-coloured sand and offers it to me. I touch the sand. It is wet. This is the height of summer and the dunes haven't seen rain in many months. Yet Chhattar Singh burrows a mere six inches and pulls out more wet sand, brandishing it like a magician who has just pulled a rabbit out of his hat.

'*Jahaan lagaav hota hai*,' he says, '*wahaan algaav bhi hota hai*.'
(Where there is attachment, there is also separation.)

Chhattar Singh can go hours without speaking a single word. But when he is in the mood, as he is now, he will impart the wisdom of the ages, gratis. Sand particles, he explains, do not coalesce like clay. When clay hardens, it cracks, allowing moisture to escape. Sand particles, on the other hand, stay separate and do not harden or fissure. Hence, the moisture that has seeped into the dune does not escape. The heart of the dune, a few feet deep, is a water-storing miracle.

We slip and slide to the bottom of the dune, and there Chhattar Singh points to a hand-dug well brimming with water in the deep Thar, in spite of months of drought. The *beri*, a percolation well, sucks the water from the belly of the dune, drop by clean, fresh, filtered drop. I look around and see a line of beris along the base of that dune.

It is a masterclass in the art of survival. Those who live in the deep desert know to check for a hint of moisture in a dune. Finding wet sand at the peak of a dune is a clue that a beri dug at its base will yield life-giving water. It is old knowledge: in centuries past, when the Silk Road was a thriving artery of global commerce, such beris served as lifelines for merchants from Samarkand and Persia who traversed the Thar to reach Jaisalmer, a vital trading post.

The secret of these magic wells lies in geology. The subcutaneous layer of the desert is gypsum, a mineral with a calcium base that is widely used as the main component of plaster and drywall. This hard layer holds the fresh rainwater and prevents it from sinking deep into the water table, which is often salty. This water, which is neither surface water nor fossil water, is called *rejwani pani*.[1]

Shepherds who graze their flocks among the dunes depend on rejwani pani. They know where to make beris, how to use them, and that it is important to ensure they are not overused or depleted. They know when to linger at a beri and when to move on. They understand that the beris must be given time to recharge. They know also to recognize the invisible borders beyond which there is no rejwani pani, where all you can find is fossil water. Few permanent settlements will be built in such places.

Deep in the desert, beyond the gypsum belts and very close to India's border with Pakistan, there are no beris, only fossil water wells. Each hand-dug well is one metre wide, plunging 200–300 metres into the bowels of the desert. The creation of these wells is a dangerous undertaking, as sand caves in easily and the walls of a newly hand-dug well can collapse as the digger bores down. Chhattar Singh, whose father has dug many such wells, recounts tales of near escapes, of wells with men still buried in them. These wells, known to the locals as *patali kuan* – literally a Hadean well, a well to Hell – provides vital subsistence to desert dwellers.

Chandar Kunwar's extended family is camped in a sand bowl not far from the border. It is a temporary settlement from where they graze their flock; they are from Seuwa, a village about forty kilometres due south. If you search for 'Seuwa' on Google Maps, you will see an extended region that includes these temporary pastoral settlements in the sands and the main village. Their camp is built near a patali kuan, worked by two camels and home to numerous little bats.

Getting water out of the depths of this Hadean well is a process as old as thirst itself. Two camels are hitched to one end of a very long rope; the other end goes over a pulley and is attached to a massive leather bag. The shepherd working the well drops into it the bag, which goes down 200 metres and fills up. At a signal, the camels walk forward, dragging the bag all the way up. The shepherd utters a signature chant – a loud call, sometimes a snatch of song – when the bag reaches the lip of the well. The camels stop on cue; the water pours out of the bag into large stone vats. By mid-morning, hundreds upon hundreds of sheep, goats and cows descend the dunes and arrive at the vats for a drink.

Now the shepherd changes his tune. This is the signal for the rope to be released. Freed from the yoke connecting the camels and weighted down by the bag, the rope rushes back through the sand, streaming a vapour trail of dust in its wake. The shepherd grasps the end of the rope at the last split second to stop it from disappearing into the well. The camels walk back and get hitched to the rope again. It is a mesmeric performance of coordination, precision, strength, timing – the secret to the survival of shepherds and their flocks alike.

I watch the shepherd – dressed in a white vest and dhoti, his skin burnt ebony from sun exposure, a shock of curly hair filled with blowing sand – time his grab at the end of the rope to the very last moment, and wonder: *Has the rope ever disappeared into the well, taking the bag with it?* 'Have you,' asks Chhattar Singh, 'ever allowed your camera to slip from your hands?'

I join the sheep at the watering trough, sip some of the water I scoop up in my cupped hands. It is drinkable, with a hint – no more – of salt. Unlike the beri which depends on percolation, the water level in the patali kuan never rises or ebbs. These wells tap into deep aquifers. The one we observe is at least a hundred years old; another, in a village further into the desert, is over 700 years old.

Chhattar Singh and I join the shepherds in drinking chai made with sheep's milk, the creamiest milk I have ever tasted. Camel's milk, they tell me, runs the thinnest. A shepherd slaps and kneads a pound of wheat into a *rota*, the thick flatbread that keeps them going when they walk the desert, and sticks it into a pit filled with sheep-dung coals.

Nawab Din joins us, dressed in flowing white long, loose robes with a large matching hand-wound turban on his head, sporting a heavy beard, and customary pointy-toed dark leather *juttis* on his feet. He leans his walking stick against a wall, takes a cloth bundle off his shoulder and sits down by the well. He is a trader, here to pick up the flock he had ordered eight months ago. He will collect the 400 sheep he has paid for, and truck them to the abattoirs of Amritsar and Delhi. 'This meat is *garam*,' he says. High in calories. It is in great demand across northern India, and even in Hyderabad in the south, as it is supposed to be ideal for biryani.

As the sheep file past him to the watering trough, Nawab Din pats them on the back to gauge their health and the quality of their meat. That is all it takes for him to judge whether they've been sick in the intervening months, whether their meat will fetch a good price. His quality check is a matter of course – he has already committed to the buy and will take them all anyway, irrespective of their health.

The two shepherds work the well; Nawab Din chooses his 400 sheep; a small boy carries a newborn lamb to its mother to nurse; and Chhattar Singh sits down beside me, in the mood to teach.

Every village in this area, he says, is planned around water. When done right, each village will have access to all three types of water: *palar pani*, surface water harvested from rain on the *aagor* (catchment); rejwani pani, percolated, or capillary water siphoned by beris; and patali pani, the deep water table reached by the kuans. This way, no single source will get overused and run dry.

Which water gets used when is governed by a natural cycle. The monsoon (July–August and maybe a few sprinkles in September) and the three months after are palar pani season; once the lakes dry up, the beris come into play; in the deepest part of the Thar where there is no underlying gypsum layer and hence no beris or lakes, the kuan acts as the lifeline.

In this region of the desert, water acknowledges no divisions of religion, caste or status. Muslim and Hindu shepherds access the same lakes, the same beris. It is an inalienable rule handed down the centuries – in the desert you never deny anyone water. Beris and kuans are never on fenced-off or private lands; all water sources are community-owned. No one ever appropriates a water source for personal use.

The villagers or shepherds who dig the wells have first-use rights in times of drought – but even so, the digging of beris and kuans is a community effort. Only one person has to express intent. Creating a water source in the desert for the benefit of the community and without harming the environment is considered *punya* – sacred work. Once a member of the village expresses an intent to dig a well, the others join out of respect for the activity. They consider themselves artisans rather than workers; their work is to be respected. They expect no payment, no return for the labour they donate to the common cause. They have a word for this – *lashipa*, working for the sheer joy of creating.

This is the old way, and the reason so many beris and kuans have outlived their makers. It harks back to an ancient ethic, a centuries-old water wisdom in the deep Thar, the youngest desert in the world.

The land is the colour of burnt caramel. It is flat, featureless; there are no trees in sight, no blade of grass, no ditch, no dune, no shrub, no ups, no downs. Nothing disturbs the absolute flatness of the ground.

The ground is hard, covered in gravel the colour of burnished iron ore. Light wisps of white cirrus lift from this one-dimensional landscape and burn in the blazing sun. A wind whips up a fine dust that swirls around and creates a mid-morning heat shimmer, painting mirages on the horizon.

To the untrained eye, this is wasteland: barren, arid, infertile, uncultivable. Shepherds like Chhattar Singh traverse the district, reading the soil, identifying the vegetation, gauging the water content, seeking out ideal spots for wells and ponds and lakes, calculating the gradient of the land and how the water will flow.

We drive across the aagor, over ground burnt dark and baked hard by the relentless sun. A row of trees comes into view on the horizon, marking the beginning of the end of this catchment. Where there are trees, there probably is water. But this is May – peak summer. There is no water in sight on this large tract of land fringed at its extremities by the kheri, the feathery giving tree of the desert.

We are in a *khadeen*, a catchment area that is a collaboration between the land and its people. A khadeen is old magic.

While it is a farm, it is also much more than that. It is at once a water-harvesting structure, an oasis-like moisture-retaining structure, and an agricultural field.

Khadeens date back 700 to 900 years and are the brainchild of the Paliwal Brahmins. There is no documentation, however; their origin stories are embedded in an oral tradition handed down through generations, immortalized in *chhand* – rhythmic poetry – by itinerant minstrels of the Manganiyar community, the fabled bards of the Thar.

Their songs evoke a long-ago land of survival and betrayal; they tell of how Nasir-ud-din Mahmud Shah of the Delhi Sultanate, seduced by the fabled prosperity of Pali, descended on the city with his army in 1273 AD and laid siege. The Paliwals and their Rajput protectors, numbering in thousands, held firm, trusting in their knowledge of agriculture and water management. Mahmud Shah, who had expected an easy conquest, was furious. *How do these Brahmins survive?* he had wondered. *From where do they source water and food?*

The answer lay in a large lake, Bijhano, which supplied fresh, sweet water to the inhabitants. The Paliwals were expert agriculturists, their granaries always full. With plentiful food and a reliable water source, the settlement was in a position to withstand even the most prolonged siege.

Mahmud Shah now decided to turn this strength into a fatal weakness. He ordered quantities of rich *geru* (red oxide) powder to be dumped in the lake. When the residents of Pali, who were strict vegetarians, found the colour of blood in their water, their rage knew no bounds. Throwing the city gates open, they – Brahmins and sadhus and Rajputs, all – rushed out in the hundreds of thousands against the Shah's troops, embracing certain death under the full moon of Raksha Bandhan.

Very few survived the carnage. One such, featuring prominently in the songs of the Manganiyars, was Kadhan. Even though he does not know how many perished in the suicidal charge, he has heard that the *janeu*, sacred threads of the dead Brahmins, collected together weighed eight maunds (320 kilograms).

The handful of survivors fled west and dispersed among eighty-four villages, called *kheras*, in and around Jaisalmer. Here they made a home for themselves and rebuilt their lives from scratch. They came to be called the Pali-walas – Brahmins from Pali. At the helm of one such group of survivors, Kadhan roamed the desert and finally settled in the village of Kuldhara (in today's Jaisalmer district). Drawing on the knowledge of his tribe, he set to work to create a lake that would sustain the survivors. He named it Udhansar and built several khadeens in appropriate locations close to the lake.

The khadeen is the Paliwal's secret to not only surviving, but thriving in the unforgiving desert. Kadhan knows how to read the soil, the gradients of the land, the wind and the weather; he knows where and how to find hidden water – it is a generational knowledge. His khadeens facilitate kharif and rabi crops, sugarcane, wheat, guar, bajra – enough to feed the whole khera without harming the land. The excess crop will bring in money from trade.

Kadhan squats on the *dhora*, a three-to-four-metre-high bund, of his dry khadeen and looks eastward in the direction of Pali, the town his people had fled. He stands up, straightens his *jama* and readjusts his *khanjar* into his *kamarband*. Reaching into an inside pocket, he pulls out a small pouch of freshly procured Malwa opium of the finest quality. Pinching off a bit, he rolls it between finger and thumb into a small ball, sticks it under his tongue and begins walking the length of his newly prepared dhora. He appraises the gentle upward slope of the flat, empty, hard aagor and decides he has read the land correctly.

He waits for the rains. The soil in the khadeen, significantly different in composition from that of the aagor, allows water to seep beneath the surface. The earth will drink deep, saturating itself slowly over a space of two months. It will then be ready to accept the seeds. Kadhan and his fellow farmers will sow wheat, two kinds of mustard, gram, herbs and guar bean to reap in the winter. To do this, they will not need a single drop of water other than that one spell of rain which, thanks to the knowledge they have acquired over centuries, will make the soil moist and fertile.

The rain that rolls down the gentle slope brings with it sheep, goat and cow poop from the aagor, which fertilizes the land. Successive seasons of farming leaves the land richer and more fecund. Farming the khadeen way is a matter of being gentle with the land, understanding the nature of it, and optimizing it to derive maximum benefit from minimal rainfall. Across the centuries after their flight from Pali, the descendants of Kadhan and the other surviving Paliwals grew rich beyond imagination.

Seven hundred and forty-one years later, in 2013, I stand with Chhattar Singh atop a dhora and listen entranced as he brings the story of Kadhan and the Paliwals to vivid life. We overlook an ancient khadeen that stretches out in front of us. The deep depression spreads over many acres and nestles in the curve of the ten-foot-high dhora, fortified over centuries by desert sandstone.

The ground, drier than bone, cracked and broken and scarred, waits patiently for rain that will arrive at some point during the southwest monsoon season. On average, the region gets roughly 80–100 millimetres – a thimbleful compared to the south Indian state of Kerala, which is somewhat smaller in area than Jaisalmer district but receives a whopping 3,000 millimetres of monsoon rain on average.

A few millimetres of rain is all that Chhattar Singh, with his understanding of the land, needs. That rain will travel down the aagor and come to rest in the depression hemmed in by the dhoras.

A group of men walk across the khadeen towards us. 'Look at his face,' says Chhattar Singh, pointing in the direction of a wan young man of slight build, unwashed hands poking out from grimy blue shirtsleeves, a shock of sand-caked hair standing all on end. 'There is no water in it. He is like the God of Death.'

The young man is the first to reach Chhattar Singh. His eyes shift from Chhattar to me and back again, and then they fall. 'Mohan Ram is a Bhil,' says Chhattar Singh by way of introduction, 'and he has chosen the curse.'

The other members of the group have caught up with him by now. A tall, wiry man in a spotless white kurta-pyjama greets Chhattar Singh warmly. This is Gaji Ram, another Bhil; he is accompanied by his three sons, all in their early twenties and dressed in smart pants and T-shirts, with smiles on their faces and ceremonial red threads – acquired at some recent festival – around their wrists. They nod in agreement as Chhattar Singh relates, for my benefit, the story of the Bhils' curse.

One evening, Parvati and her consort Shiva looked down on the Bhils from their abode high up in the mountains. Moved by their plight and wishing to help her brothers, Parvati sweet-talked Shiva into putting a silver pot in their path as the Bhils returned home for the night. The Bhils walked past the pot without so much as noticing it. Shiva smirked, but Parvati wasn't giving up just yet. She presented them with a majestic bull – none other than the sacred Nandi who, she told her brothers, would help lift them out of poverty.

The Bhils thought the bull would magically improve their lives. When no such thing happened, they wondered if Parvati had meant that there was treasure to be found inside the bull. So they killed it. When she heard of the bull's slaying, Parvati was enraged. 'Since you have killed a beautiful, sacred creature,' she raged, 'you will never amount to much in farming!'

Believing the curse to be true, generations of Bhils have adopted fatalism. 'There is no point in working since we are cursed' is the pervasive mindset. Mohan Ram, squatting nearby, his grimy fingers tugging a blade of grass loose from the baked earth and twirling it abstractedly, is of a similar opinion. Chhattar Singh says dismissively, almost with contempt, 'He has chosen the curse.'

July draws to a close. The rain is over two weeks late and Gaji Ram feels the beginnings of despair. He has followed Chhattar Singh's precepts to the letter. He first prepped his dhora by piling thorny bushes against it, allowing the howling desert winds of summer to pile sand high and create a natural bund. The dhora is now ready, and the khadeen awaits the rains that do not come.

In the desert, it rains in bands. Typically each band is about five kilometres wide, with intervals of five to seven kilometres between bands. We hear that one such band has arrived at a point further south, the rain coming down in thick veils. Over tea, as the wind howls outside, Chhattar Singh recalls the previous year when a village on one side of the road received rainfall while a *dhaani* (village outpost) on the other side remained dry. One village saw a bumper crop, the other remained arid. Desert rain is mercurial, he says. All you can do is prepare your khadeen and hope.

Gaji Ram was not always a farmer. He is a Bhil, one of the accursed. He had been jailed once on false charges of maiming a cow. He has callused hands from a stint as a road labourer, and has known what it is like to hold a begging bowl. He believed in the curse then, his self-esteem at an all-time low.

The agent of change was his uncle, Khamana Ram, who believed in neither curses nor fate. Instead, he put his faith in

Chhattar Singh's knowledge and proclivity for hard work – the combination had made him rich. On his deathbed, Khamana Ram had given his nephew one piece of advice: 'Listen to Chhattar Singh and do as he says.'

Though the moribund suggestion left a strong imprint in his mind, Gaji Ram did not turn into a believer overnight. Chhattar Singh spent his own money on diesel for Gaji's Ram's tractor but he, with a Bhil's sense of destiny, chose to leave the engine running all night, burning up the fuel so that his benefactor would think that he had actually been working on the farm.

The wise Chhattar Singh did not persist. He could have taken over and done the work himself, but that was not his way. Over time and endless sessions of bantal, Chhattar Singh taught Gaji to believe in himself, to believe that change was possible. 'My doing their work will not bring sustenance,' he now tells me. 'It has to come from within. They need to be prepared to put in the hard work for a khadeen – or anything for that matter – to be a success. We need to change the handouts-and-aid mindset.'

In time, Gaji Ram came around. By 2010, he and his three sons had built a dhora, the initial step towards a khadeen. In the first year, they reaped handsome harvests of gram, wheat and mustard, earning in excess of ₹4 lakh each – a princely sum for a family used to living hand-to-mouth.

Motivated at last and brimming with self-confidence, Gaji Ram and his family have worked tirelessly through the summer, preparing his dhora. And now they wait, first in hope and then, as the rains keep away, with a growing sense of trepidation and that familiar feeling of fatalism.

We are well into August. The rest of India is either celebrating bountiful monsoons or ruing terrible floods. Gaji Ram's strip of desert remains as dry as camel poop on a sand dune.

Then, early in the morning of 15 August, the clouds come rolling in over the aagors and bombard the land with rain. Over 100 millimetres – more than the desert has seen in previous years – falls in just a few hours. 'It won't stop,' a panicked Gaji Ram reports to Chhattar Singh on the phone. 'My dhora will burst – I'll be ruined. What do I do?'

But the dhora holds; his khadeen floods, as do all other khadeens in the district. Ten days after the initial cloudburst, the rain continues to pour, flowing from the catchment area into Gaji Ram's khadeen. The desert turns to marsh, and birds of all kinds flock to it.

Chhattar Singh accompanies Gaji Ram and his sons on a walk around the khadeen, animatedly discussing the deluge. 'The water came up to here,' they say, pointing to where the washback shows clearly, a broad-brush muddy brown stripe against the side of the dhora, thick with sundry vegetation left behind by the retreating water. *Vaazh*, they call it, the mark of the highest level of water. They will use it to calibrate their dhoras and *chaadars* (canals) for the next season.

As he inspects the dhora for possible weaknesses and discusses his plans with Chhattar Singh, Gaji Ram laughs heartily. His voice rises an octave with excitement; he is filled with a renewed sense of possibility, with refurbished belief in the ancient wisdom of the land.

There is much 'water in his face'.

THE LANDSCAPE OF LOSS

It is through the power of observation, the gifts of eye and ear, of tongue and nose and finger, that a place first rises up in our mind; afterward it is memory that carries the place, that allows it to grow in depth and complexity. For as long as our records go back, we have held these two things dear, landscape and memory. Each infuses us with a different kind of life.

The one feeds us, figuratively and literally. The other protects us from lies and tyranny.

BARRY LOPEZ,
About This Life[1]

THE HORIZON FLASHES INTERMITTENT NEON IN THE DARK, silhouetting ghostly clouds.

'Those scattered clouds are called *kanthi*,' Chhattar Singh says. 'If they come together with the promise of rain, they will change to *ghataatope*. And should the clouds become very dense, they will be called *kalaan*.'

That night, the kanthi does not build. It does not rain.

As life stirs awake the next morning, Chhattar Singh and I sit with cups of chai and watch the wind ripple through a feathery, fruit-laden khejri tree. He points to the tufts of white cloud trailing in arcs and lines all the way to the horizon. '*Teetar pankhi*,' he says. The analogy is breathtakingly apt – the wispy clouds are, I notice, akin to the patterns on the primary feathers of a partridge.

I am tempted to ask Chhattar Singh to cycle through the names the desert people have for various types of clouds. But language does not work that way; it is not learned overnight. You need to invest time and patience to listen, to observe, to see and touch and feel, to experience the land with all your senses.

A soft, warm wind picks up. The teetar pankhi clouds flock together into a light cottony blanket overhead. They have a name for that too. *Paans.*

It is said that the Inuit people of the Arctic region have forty names for snow – which makes sense, since they are surrounded by snow all year and have an intimate acquaintance with all its variations. The people of the Thar get only forty cloudy days in a year, and yet they have as many names for clouds.

The deep western part of the Thar desert lies in Jaisalmer district. It is bounded in the north and west by Pakistan, in the east by Jodhpur, with Barmer to the south and Bikaner to the northeast. The average rainfall is a meagre 100 millimetres in a good year, about a tenth of the national average and a pitiful 2 per cent of the rainfall Kerala and some of the wettest areas in India receive. For the people of the Thar, a sighting of clouds is a memorable event, worth commemorating in a special lexicon, as these moments hold the key to their very existence.

Traditional desert dwellers, many of whom are shepherds, have an intimate knowledge of this vast and differentiated land. They map it not in kilometres but on a much more minute scale. The land slopes gently, barely perceptible to us used to hurtling around in motorized vehicles, rising about a foot over a kilometre.

Yet these barefoot geographers can sense and use this incline to great effect.

We head southwards from the village we are in, under *eyloor* skies. Kair trees are in full bloom; some have begun to bear fruit. A babbler pokes its beak eye-deep into the coral-coloured kair flower for its nectar, a natural sweetener widely used in the local cuisine. A whistling wind bends the branches of a khejri tree, feathery and laden with long pods of *sangri* fruit. A husband and wife, camel cart in tow, harvest the fruit with long hooks.

The caper-like kair fruit and the fruit of the khejri tree, sangri, are invaluable additions to a summer menu. In the months before the rains, shepherds also harvest *pilu*, the tiny fruit of the *jaal* tree. A mid-summer walk with Chhattar Singh includes frequent halts under jaals to pick and eat pilu, which look like tiny, perfectly round grapes, red when ripe, with a subtle sweetness minus the tartness of the fruit it resembles.

Mushrooms that grow under the *lana* plant in the monsoons are a delicacy, to be carefully harvested and savoured. Further into the sandy saline desert, orange buds of the *phog* plant are mixed with curd in winter for *baata*, a kind of raita. The lana flowers are mixed into winter rotis. Milk – derived from cows, goats, sheep and camels – buttermilk and ghee accompany the fruits.

A desert family, eating the traditional way, will never want for food. Wheat and millet come from khadeens, supplemented with fruit from the commons as per the gifts of the season. Until recently, dwellers in the deep desert had not seen potatoes or cauliflowers, French beans or sugar – and no one suffered from diabetes.

Chhattar Singh waves us off the road and over scree, for which too he has a name – *magra*. *Chinkaras*[2] dart away from our vehicle, then wheel about and watch us from a distance. In season, it is reportedly common to see mating pairs of godawn, the highly endangered great Indian bustard.

We stop. The ground is now smooth sandstone layered in purple and gold, orange and burgundy. And out of the blue, there is water.

It takes a while to fathom the source of these pools that materialize in the midst of layered rock. Rainwater, percolating through the porous rock further up, has dripped onto stone, whittling it over aeons into a natural cistern. It is several feet deep in some places, and shallow enough in others that we can see through to the rock bed. It is full of freshwater. I kneel, cup my hands, and sip. The water is sweet, strained of impurities by the rock.

The desert people call it a *bhey*. Unsearchable on Google Maps, these are remembered lifelines, paths to water sources that only the shepherds know, just as they know where the sevan grass ends and the phog plants begin, or how to reach the one area where dune after dune of murat grass can be found. Shepherds pridefully point out that the desert carries in its womb thirty-six types of seeds awaiting *dharolyuo*, the joyous veil of rain that bridges sky and earth and brings forth vegetation.

Desert dwellers recognize borders observed by birds, outlines that are thoughtful, meaningful, natural – inspired by geology. With no written documentation to guide them, they rely on memory and muscle, on a visceral interaction with the land, and they are one with it.

These memories – composed of knowledge – are passed on through words – place names and named phenomena, songs and symbols. The act of naming – *chhinto* for a drizzle, *ghutyo*[3] for the asphyxiating stillness of clouds that blanket the sky without giving way to rain – is an act of homage, of recognizing worth and according importance to all that holds the key to survival.

These ambling geographers, these *mojri-* and *saafa*-clad ecologists, read the land and know how to 'divine' water. They can tell *ubrelyo* from *dhundh*, follow the *baaval*, towards as yet unseen kalaan, identify over eighty different desert species of plants from *aak* to *zillon*, and anticipate the behaviours of sandgrouse and spiny-tailed lizard, chinkara and bustard.

The people of the desert are archivists and cartographers of their landscape. Theirs is a lived, intensely local knowledge. Desert dwellers invent words for what they see and experience; these words enter the lexicon and are passed on orally as individual knowledge grows into collective knowledge.

'My son doesn't speak this language …' Chhattar Singh's voice trails off. He who has words for every natural phenomenon is at a loss when it comes to describing the sadness of a passing era, the ineffable erosion of memory.

Narendra, the youngest of his three sons, is in middle school. Modern education in this state, as in many others across India, is wholly disconnected from the geography, biology, zoology, hydrology, geomorphology and anthropology of the land in which it is imparted. The children of Chhattar Singh's village can draw maps of India, but not of their own district or village. They cannot tell rejwani pani from patali pani. The lived language of the desert has been replaced with a universal, theoretical knowledge of nowhere in particular, administered indiscriminately to all as per the diktat of a distant Delhi.

'Education today,' says Chhattar Singh in a flat, carefully emotionless tone, 'is training my son, and kids like him, to become slaves of the 31st' – that is, pay day.

The time I spend with Chhattar Singh and his peers confirms my growing sense that all over the country deep knowledge of the land is declining with each generation, the value of such knowledge being officially undermined.

When we lose an evocative lexicon, when we forget the organic words and their import, we lose what Barry Lopez calls the 'voice of memory over the land'. When this happens – and it is happening throughout – the land risks losing its defenders, its most passionate advocates. With this comes the concomitant danger of land being appropriated by those who are not familiar with it, by interlopers who don't know where the last surface water can be found or how to harvest rain or that seeds lie dormant under the sands; by engineers or forest department officials who may not be equipped to recognize that desert dunes are, in fact, disguised water wells.

This forgetting has meant that the deep Thar, home to Chhattar Singh and his rich, varied lexicon, has now been condemned as a 'wasteland' and reduced, by these same interlopers, to a 'resource', a commodity for sale.

Northwest of Jaisalmer, gobs of rough gravel in metre-high mounds flank a road strung taut between swathes of the Thar. An ashen haze obscures the path ahead; the occasional lorry, laden with gravel well past its carrying capacity, lumbers out of it, trailing black noxious fumes out of its exhaust pipes.

From deep within this all-encompassing smog rises a hellish din, as if a thousand vessels are being banged together in a cacophony. At the heart of that smog – the source of the noise, the dust, the lorries scurrying to and fro – is a cement factory.

The gobs of gravel dotting the landscape are mounds of limestone. By some estimates, eight million metric tons are scooped out of the Thar each year. Lorries cart the gravel into factories where it is processed, and then carried east to the steel plants of Bokaro and Bhilai, Jamshedpur and Rourkela – slag for shining steel cities.

In a landmark case that ran from 1982 to 1988, the Supreme Court of India ruled against limestone quarrying in the lower Himalaya. The mines that hollowed out the Dehradun valley were declared illegal under the Forest Conservation Act. The Supreme Court went a step further and ordered the restoration of the forests in the valley. Then, in 1991, the apex court, while deliberating on the pollution discharged by mines and industrial units, observed that a clean environment is in fact a fundamental right. As we motor though the haze of dust, so dense that it infiltrates the insides of our car even with the windows all rolled up, I recall the court deeming that the right to life, a fundamental right under Article 21 of the Constitution of India, includes the right to enjoy pollution-free water and air.

Consequently, the Government of India sent a technical team to seek out alternate sources of limestone. They found it in the deserts north of Jaisalmer: high-quality limestone, low in silica, perfectly suited for the country's burgeoning steel industry. Bonus: no forests in the area for the Supreme Court to champion.

In 1985, the National Wasteland Development Board was formed to bring 'wastelands in the country into productive use through a massive programme of afforestation and tree plantations' and for 'improving land productivity'. Subscribing to an outdated, colonial, way of thinking, they issue the 'Wasteland Atlas of India' every few years. These atlases define 'wasteland' thus: 'Degraded land which can be brought under vegetative cover, with reasonable effort, and which is currently under-utilised and land which is deteriorating for lack of appropriate water and soil management or on account of natural causes.'

Going by this definition, 68 per cent of Jaisalmer district was deemed a 'wasteland'. In 1988, the government began 'open-cast mining with a single bench and deep hole blasting' in the Thar, to 'better utilize' it.[4]

The *khann* killed the aagor. 'Why couldn't they ask us before setting up their mines?' ask bewildered locals. Khadeens and beris in proximity to the mines have gone dry, depriving denizens of traditional food and water sources and making them dependent on the government's piped water. They refer to the '*nahar ka pani*', the water of the canal, with a grimace of disgust. It is toxic, they say; it reeks, and is virtually unusable.

That, however, is not how the government sees it. As per the government of Rajasthan, the 'Indira Gandhi Nahar Project (IGNP) is one of the most gigantic projects in the world aiming to de-desertify and transform desert wasteland into agriculturally productive area'. The tail end of the main canal of the 'nahar', as the Indira Gandhi canal is known in the western Thar, reached Ramgarh in 1992. Carrying water from the valleys of Punjab, the main canal branched into intermediate ones which then forked into even smaller canals snaking through to the deep heart of the Thar. Under Phase II of the IGNP, over 4,000 square kilometres of desert were to be 'utilized' for irrigated agriculture.

But the water never made it that far. And where the water did reach, the result was vastly contrary to the government's grandiose vision of a green desert. In the main canal near Ramgarh, intensive irrigation raised the water table and increased salinity, rendering large 'de-desertified areas' waterlogged and useless. Where once native grasses grew, brilliant agamas scuttled, butterflies drank deep from bright yellow heliotropiums and desert foxes darted on spindly legs, there is now nothing. A desert wind howls mockingly over an arid dustbowl.

Back then, the government had sold dreams of irrigation to about 1,000 local landless farmers, each of whom received about six acres. Those farmers stand today on wasted land, holding useless pieces of paper and sinking into deepening holes of debt. The government allotted desert land further into the Thar to 700 families displaced by the Pong Dam in Himachal Pradesh, but the canals do not carry water to these areas. One family went, took a look at the land, and left.

And then there are mosquitoes. No one had heard of them until 1990, when the first malaria epidemic broke out. *Plasmodium falciparum*, the deadly malarial parasite, thrived in the stagnant waters of the nahar. Today the district records the highest incidence of malaria in Rajasthan. Every family has at least one sufferer. More recently, dengue has been added to their plethora of woes. The canal brought in other pests like the highly invasive *bawliya*, which blanketed the land and sucked it dry, not to mention the crop-raiding nilgai and wild boar, neither of which belongs in the deep desert.

In the villages I walk through, I see squat yellow tanks of nahar ka pani. The supply is irregular; the water makes an appearance once every three days or so. Women use it to wash clothes, but never for consumption. It stinks, they say, crinkling their noses.

Carcasses of animals have been seen floating in the canal, and this same water comes through, after rudimentary filtration, to the villages. The filters don't carry away the smell, nor does it rid the water of parasites. Locals complain that they fall ill from drinking nahar ka pani. They prefer the beri – their clean, fresh, reliable, traditional percolation well – that provides water all through the year. No one has ever fallen sick from drinking 'beri ka pani'.

'De-desertifying' had another devastating effect on the landscape – it cleared the grassland commons for agriculture. Vast swathes of native grasses such as the sevan and the endemic phog were razed from the roots up and burned. These plants sustained millions of goat and sheep – the mainstay of the people of the desert. As waterlogging rendered the land unproductive, the desert was damned twice: it not only lost its native vegetation but was also deprived of the ability to regenerate itself.

The area has now truly become a 'wasteland'; the government's much-hyped canal has created the very condition it wrongly diagnosed and sought to cure. The smaller canals are bone-dry, throttled by sand. And yet, amidst these half-buried legacies of the government's miscalculation, the desert slowly rejuvenates itself; shepherds graze their flocks, grasses begin to thrive, a fox darts off in the distance, and a brisk wind blows the sand about.

An *oran*, in this part of the Thar, is a sacred grove – a stretch of indigenous trees that belong to, and are protected by, the local community. No one is allowed to hack even a branch of these trees or till a single square inch of the oran.

Orans made of jaal, bordi and kair trees line the road from Jaisalmer to Ramgarh. In some places, these stretches are five kilometres long and thirty-five kilometres deep – sparse forests of tree after sacred tree. These orans are unrecorded, Chhattar Singh tells me, and so the government could do with them as it pleased. It decided to farm wind energy here – digging deep holes, erecting huge fans and farming the wind to reap carbon credits.

The area we are in has the highest number of windmills in this part of the Thar. '*Woh dekho*,' Chhattar Singh exclaims, '*giddh maraa hua!*[5] We slam to a halt. I see a wing on the ground. About two metres away lies the rest of the griffon vulture, slashed in two by the churning blades of a windmill.

From this point on, it is a bloody game of hopscotch. This windmill clean, the next with blood on its blades; another sparkling, followed by one that has gutted another griffon. I count six dead vultures across fifteen windmills. Babu Singh, a shepherd, waves one arm round and round. '*Khainch leta hai unko* – it sucks the birds in.' I kneel beside the carcass of a raptor and look into its vacant eye sockets. Above me, like a doom-laden soundtrack, the remorseless blades continue to grind the air in a deafening monotonous rhythm.

Slightly west of the windmills rise high dunes topped by amethyst crowns of the exotic Israeli acacia. The mandarins of the forest department, ignorant of the land and its native species, had planted these trees on top of the dunes as part of the government's afforestation mandate. The fast-growing trees now wreak havoc, tapping into the moisture-filled heart of the dunes, leeching away the desert's hidden water and drying up the beris. All across the Thar, there are signs of interlopers playing havoc with an ecosystem they have not made an effort to understand.

Near the border between India and Pakistan, the roads are smooth and well maintained – but they are raised three feet from the surrounding desert. Knifing through catchments, their height impedes the natural flow of water down a gradient to the village lakes, which are crucial for the replenishment of beris and khadeens.

The natives of this land walk. A lot. Every day. They know every dip and rise; each gradient is mapped; heights marked with intricately carved pillars. The rain, whatever little does fall, strikes this higher catchment land, the aagor, first. The water rolls down gentle inclines to collect in the depressions that are the khadeens, or lakes. There are beris in these depressions which will serve communities long after the lakes have evaporated.

Vital to these water sources is the high land. Chhattar Singh leans forward in his seat. 'This was once an aagor,' he sighs, 'until the road knifed through.' The gradient carried rain into a village lake, but not anymore. The height of the road we are on means that the water can no longer flow from east to west towards the khadeen.

As we crisscross Jaisalmer district, we continuously encounter two different worlds. In one lives a people grounded, observant, wise to the magic and the limitations of the desert, and therefore able to survive, even thrive, in a seemingly hostile environment. In the other lives officialdom – a hodgepodge of 'departments' and 'bureaus', unaware of the intricacies of the land, intent on imposing their will on an ecosystem they continue to misunderstand.

I think of the fable of the six blind men and the elephant, and I reimagine it for our times. One touches the limestone and thinks, *Ah, a resource to be mined!* Another feels the wind that sweeps the desert into dunes and says, *Oh yes, carbon brownie points for the taking!* A third feels the dryness of the sand and envisions a world of intricate canals and flourishing agriculture, and a fourth dreams of large stretches of acacia on the towering dunes …

Each touches an element of the desert at some opportunistic point and fashions his worldview accordingly; none bothers to fathom the desert in its intricate entirety and, therefore, none appreciates how an intervention here could ruin an integral dynamic elsewhere.

As the blind men come to blows over their individual interpretations, a sighted man comes along and tells them of the complex living, breathing creature they have failed to comprehend as a whole. And the blind men listen as their limited knowledge is gradually replaced with a gently growing awareness.

In the here and now of the desert, though, the fable has a grim denouement. There are the sighted, the viscerally aware, like Chhattar Singh or Babu Singh or any number of people who walk this land. They speak eloquently, with the benefit of deep observation and a keen sense of the totality of a desert far greater, far more nuanced than its individual parts.

Chhattar Singh looks up at the pile of clouds rising high into the sky. To the poetic eye of the desert dweller, the shape resembles a woman balancing a water pot on her head. They have a name for this cloud formation too – *pani hari*, water bearers. '*Yeh drishya ka roop hai*,' Chhattar Singh murmurs, '*bhaasha nahi*.' This is a manifestation of the land, not a language.

His own son would not know the name, nor understand the subtleties Chhattar Singh sees in the sky. The loss of a landscape lexicon is more acute than just the vanishing of words – it foreshadows a time when the elemental connections between the land and its people will be severed. It plunges us into a blindness that is total, wilful, destructive – the blindness of those who refuse to see.

पाँख

PART 2

VEINS OF OUR LAND

IN THE SHIFTING EMBRACE OF THE GANGA

I AM IN PANCHANANDAPUR, ON THE BANKS OF THE RIVER GANGA in the Indian state of West Bengal. It is the monsoon season, and nothing is as I remember it from my previous trips.

The tea stall that I used to frequent with Tarikul-bhai, my friend and guide for all things related to the Ganga in these parts, is three-quarters submerged. The ferry landings are fully underwater, forcing people to wade waist-deep to reach dry land. The river has risen at least ten feet higher, maybe more, than her level in the dry season.

Ten-wheeler trucks, half sunken in the river, are loading up on raw jute offloaded from large barges that have come from up and down the river. Men, women and youth, many sporting conical cane hats against the fierce sun, are harvesting and curing jute everywhere. On every water body, from the tiniest *pukur*, or pond, to the biggest river, cut jute floats on rafts weighed down by dung or mud. After a couple of weeks of soaking, they will strip the fibre from the central stick and dry it for use in fabric, bags and braided ropes. The sticks will be burned as fuel.

Tarikul-bhai has booked a fishing boat to take us upstream

to the head of the delta. The Ganga is no longer the green-blue aquamarine of my summer memories; rather, we seem to be floating in a rimless bowl of tea. The sky – featureless, clad in a thick shawl of white clouds – covers us like a cloche. The sun is nowhere to be seen, but the reflected glare of its light is blinding.

Floating under that cloche in our boat, it is as if we are being slowly steamed. On this windless morning, rivulets of perspiration run down our faces and backs. Clumps of hyacinth, that invasive scourge of all wetlands in India, float by, sometimes wearing pretty purple flowers or bobbing under the weight of grey wagtails or Asian pied starlings. Occasionally a boat, ferrying men, women, children, goats, motorcycles, cars, bicycles and even a cow, passes by on the horizon, breaking the monotony of the expanse of turgid, tea-brown waters.

To our right, the river eddies viciously with large circular currents called *ghurnis*. After an animated discussion with the boatman in Bengali, Tarikul-bhai gives me the consensus view: 'Bhangan is imminent wherever this current reaches'. He uses the local word *bhangan* for the breaking of soil. This kind of breakage can destroy and drown acres of land within minutes.

We float past what look like large swathes of marshes but in reality are the tops of vegetation growing on submerged silt islands. Tall *Saccharum* grasses, cattle fodder, even trees, are more under the water than above it. A grave-faced, massive, endangered[1] greater adjutant stork lifts off from the vegetation and is joined by its mate.

I scan the waters for more signs of life. Somewhere inside this tea soup there is likely to be long-snouted, sharp-toothed, blind, side-swimming Gangetic dolphins – among the oldest cetaceans[2] in the world, which have adapted to the murky, silty rivers of the Ganga–Brahmaputra basin. Somewhere upstream I am likely to see, basking on sandbanks, even longer-snouted, exclusively fish-eating crocodilians called *gharials*.[3]

Both species are embedded in Indian mythology and in the local consciousness; they are, it is believed, the vehicles of the Ganga in her Goddess form. Every temple along the riverbanks dedicated to the Goddess shows her riding on the 'makara'[4] – a composite gharial–dolphin creature. And both species are highly endangered.

As we near a marsh, I ask the boatman to cut the motor. Drifting with the current, with no other boat or settlement in sight, I feel for a brief few moments the raw embrace of this river – the holiest of them all, the spiritually purest, the remover of sins, the redeemer of souls. All across the Indian subcontinent, for thousands of years, every devout Hindu regardless of caste and creed has aspired to touch, sip, bathe in the Ganga at least once in their lifetime.

I trail my hand in her waters to feel, in a visceral way, her unstoppable power, her speed, spontaneity, playfulness, wilfulness, her life-giving benevolence and her devastating waywardness. In that moment, I am struck by the immense potency that this deified river – not a deity enshrined in cold stone inside a temple, but one that is alive and accessible, mutable and moody, generous and vengeful, welcoming and overwhelming all at once – has over a billion people.

We have drifted downstream; the boatman revs up the engine, jolting me out of my reverie. We continue upstream. The monsoon-swollen river is everywhere, and I remind myself that this flood is not a bad thing in and of itself. The Bengali word for the monsoons is *barshakal*, implying a regular and welcome inundation, while the word for devastating flooding is *bonya*.[5]

The river brings fine silt down from the Himalayan mountains and deposits it on these plains, creating some of the most fertile agricultural lands in the world. To walk through such a silt island under cultivation is to breathe in an aroma of paddy (rice), herbs and vegetables that you never can get in much-tilled, much-fertilized industrial farmland. This cycle of flood and ebb is what sustains – has sustained for centuries – hundreds of millions of people, for this is the most populated river delta in the world.

The delta was originally thickly forested, but the lure of silt-covered fertile land and the navigability and access that Bengal provided to the hinterland transformed it into a center for trade. In consequence, the forests were replaced by agricultural fields and the delta became increasingly populated as the people adapted themselves to the cycles of beneficial floods and ebbs.

Abu'l Fazl, the grand vizier of Emperor Akbar, wrote in the sixteenth century about this region of Bengal: 'The principal cultivation is rice, of which there are numerous kinds. If a single grain of each kind were collected, they would fill a large vase … As fast as the water rises, the stalks grow, so that the ear is never immersed.'[6]

A long-stemmed variety of rice (*Oryza sativa*) is grown in the swamplands, where it can withstand water eighteen to twenty feet deep. When the waters recede, the seeds are broadcast, and when the rains set in, the grass shoots up with the swell. Local varieties such as this one, long eschewed in favour of short-stemmed, high-yielding commercial paddy, are known to grow a foot in twenty-four hours. They reach heights of over twelve feet to keep pace with the swelling rivers and are harvested from boats.[7]

We chug upstream against the monsoon freshet, which is strong and fast. It takes us a couple of hours and then some to cover the fifteen miles to the head of the delta. This is where the Ganga leaves the state of Bihar and bends southward into West Bengal. On her right bank are the rocky hills of Rajmahal, a historically prominent city favoured by both Mughal emperors and the British for its unique geography. The bedrock is so strong that Rajmahal is immune to the vagaries of the meandering river.

Manikchak, on the opposite bank, has soft, pliable agricultural land, rich and giving, home to a robust population of farmers making the most of its fertility. Here the river, pregnant with silt, comes around a bend and, finding no purchase against the hard stone of the right bank, ricochets, ramming into the soft clay on the left bank.

All rivers, in their deltaic reaches, play ping-pong between banks, creating meanders. The Ganga has been eroding her banks for centuries. Writing in the late eighteenth century, Major Robert Hyde Colebrooke, who went on to become the Surveyor General of Bengal, describes how the meandering Ganga swells 'more than twenty-five feet' during seasonal floods and how the strength of the receding waters triggers erosion:

> It is not unusual to find, when the rainy season is over, large portions of the bank sunk into the channel; nay, even whole fields and plantations have been sometimes destroyed; and trees, which, with the growth of a century, had acquired strength to resist the most violent storms, have been suddenly undermined, and hurled into the stream.[8]

As a surveyor, he would go out on the river in a boat and sometimes find himself in the vicinity of a crashing bank. He compares the noise to 'the distant rumbling of artillery, or thunder'. But he describes this phenomenon as gradual, giving the locals enough time to remove their effects should they be too close to the crumbling bank.

This is a natural phenomenon. The river constantly migrates, and this migration triggers human migration in response. Professor Kalyan Rudra, chairman of the West Bengal Pollution Control Board, says, 'Himalayan rivers in their deltaic parts often move over great distances. The swatch of meander sweep is proportional to the discharge flowing through the river.'[9]

Except, the Ganga has been flagrantly flouting these limits over the last fifty years.

Anita Das, her husband, his aged mother, and the couple's ten-year-old son were at dinner that rainy night in July 2020 when it began: a thunderous rumble that seemed to emerge from deep within the bowels of the earth enveloped them, like the surround sound of doom.

Das and her family scrambled to gather whatever possessions they could lay their hands on and ran out of their little brick house in Birnagar into a scene of total chaos. Their neighbours, similarly burdened with whatever they could carry, were racing for higher ground, their screams of fear a counterpoint to the growling of the earth.

In the dark of that night, Das, her family and their neighbours dashed towards the primary school that had been designated as the temporary shelter in times of trouble. Having delivered her mother-in-law to the safety of the school premises, Das and her young son dashed back into their home to rescue whatever else they could.

Slipping and sliding in the falling rain, the people of the region gathered their goats, calves and cows, mattresses, cots, vessels, bundles of clothes, TVs, documents, pictures of their gods and goddesses ... What they could lay their hands on they deposited at the school, then they ran back for more through the ghostly gloom of the monsoon night.

They had seen signs of the impending disaster earlier that evening when the Ganga, swollen by the monsoons, began to eddy around their little village. These eddies, thick and brown with silt, are the harbingers of impending erosion – similar to the circular currents we saw from the boat.

The river in spate gradually undercut the ground beneath their homes. A big crack split the earth and a number of homes were trapped in the space between the crack and the river. The destruction was inevitable, and swift. By 3 a.m. the river had cut away the ground, and Das and her hapless neighbours watched as everything they had built and lived for vanished into the depths of the turbulent river.

'We are landlords to bed and beggars to rise,' says Tarikul-bhai, with a wry smile.

Tarikul-bhai is a resident of Panchanandapur, which is slightly to the north of Das's Birnagar, and he has witnessed such devastation multiple times over the past four decades.

Destructive erosion is a biannual event. The first iteration happens during the monsoon season, when the riverbed fills with the heavy sand brought down the course by the freshet, causing the waters to rise and swallow homes, trees and fields, schools, mosques and all else in its path. The second iteration occurs when the rains ebb and the waters recede, by which time the monsoon floods will have softened the earth, and in such deltas, the groundwater feeds the receding river. The softened banks are undercut by the flow and the land subsides, tumbling homesteads and paddy farms and cattle and sheep and the occasional unwary human being into the waters.

Manikchak, Panchanadapur, and several other places on the left bank of the Ganga lose land to erosion twice every year. 'Some people here have moved homes seventeen times in the last twenty years', says Tarikul-bhai.

It is not as if only those in close proximity to the river are affected. About four decades ago, Panchanandapur used to be a bustling town in the district of Malda in northern West Bengal, with a thriving trading port and bustling sugar mills and textile, grain and mango markets. Tarikul's friend Mohammed Inamul Haque, a sixty-seven-year-old teacher in Panchanandapur, recalls the town as it was even thirty years ago, when he was secretary of the market. 'There were 628 shops in the market,' he says. 'A lot of trade would go through Panchanandapur. I have seen the river swallow it all in front of my eyes.'

Haque owned thirty-three acres of land, which he lost to the river in eight bouts of erosion. After his eighth displacement, he sank all his remaining savings into a sturdy two-storied brick home that he built five kilometres away from the river.

That five-kilometre buffer between river and home gave him an initial sense of security – but over the years that security eroded along with the land itself as the river gulped its way closer and closer, and by the time I visited in 2022, the Ganga was flowing less than five hundred metres away from his front door.

Roughly 700,000 people live alongside this stretch of the Ganga.[10] 'This is not just my story,' Haque says as he sits on the veranda of his home and looks into the distance, where the glint of the river shines through the trees. 'Everyone here has stories like this. Some people had 200 bighas, others had 400.'

All deltaic rivers meander in their lower course, and a certain amount of erosion is inevitable. But something happened in northern West Bengal in the 1970s that triggered an abnormally deviant behaviour in the massive river – behaviour that has wreaked havoc in the lives of those hundreds of thousands who live along its banks. To understand what happened, it is necessary to first understand the course of the river.

The Ganga is born some twelve hundred kilometres away from where Tarikul-bhai and I stand looking down into its turgid waters. Two energetic streams, the Bhagirathi and the Alakananda, emerge from the glaciers of the lofty Himalayan range and tumble down through the state of Uttarakhand, in India. They meet at Devprayag, and the Ganga is born of their union.[11]

The river roars south through steep gorges, swinging west to Rishikesh, where the land begins to flatten out and the river's headlong rush slows down. The gorges open out into the plains at Haridwar, where she flows placid and slow. Hanging a left turn, she makes her way east, swelling in size as she folds into herself large Himalayan tributaries from the north – the Yamuna, the Ghagra, the Gandak and the Kosi – and the Sone from the south.

Flowing flat through the fertile Indo-Gangetic plains that form the Hindi heartland, the Ganga emerges from Bihar to bend south again into West Bengal. This bend is the head of her massive fan-shaped delta, before she joins the Bay of Bengal in a spectacular, million-tongued mouth clothed in dense mangrove forests – the Sundarban, 'beautiful forest'.

The mouth of the delta, which straddles India and Bangladesh, is the largest unbroken stand of mangrove forests in the world, home to the charismatic Royal Bengal tiger, the Gangetic and Irrawaddy dolphins, saltwater crocodiles, river sharks and the endangered masked finfoot, among others.

The river carries so much sediment that her fan can be seen as a turgid plume of water almost sixty miles beyond the coast. The resulting thickness of the sediment bed at the mouth of the river is a whopping ten miles.[12]

Some thirty thousand feet above, from the window seat of a commercial plane flying over the delta, I spotted that plume beyond Sagar Island, the last piece of land before the mighty river pours herself into the Bay of Bengal.

As legend has it, this island is where it all began.[13] The island was the home of King Sagara, a popular and benevolent ruler, and his 60,001 sons. Once, while they were performing the Ashwamedha Yagna – the horse sacrifice that when successfully completed elevates a mere king to the rank of monarch – the sacred horse went missing.

Sagara sent his sons to find the horse and they, in their arrogance, laid waste to all the lands they passed through. Eventually they reached the netherworld, where they saw the sage Kapila meditating and the sacrificial horse tied to a nearby tree.

Assuming that the sage had stolen the horse, they interrupted his meditation and smugly accused him. With one look and one word, the enraged sage reduced sixty thousand of Sagara's sons to ashes. Only one remained, and he returned to his father to tell him what had transpired.

Years later, the king's grandson travelled to the netherworld to plead with Kapila to bring his ancestors back to life or, at a minimum, restore their souls. 'Only Ganga can wash away their sins and make them immortal,' the sage replied.

Two generations of Sagara's descendants tried to appease the gods, beseeching them to send Ganga – who resides in heaven in the ablution pot of Lord Brahma – to earth. Finally, Bhagiratha, the great-great-grandson of Sagara, succeeded in persuading her to come to earth.

But there was a problem. The force of her descent from the heavens would likely be more than the earth could take. Bhagiratha did penance once again, pleading with the gods to help. Brahma, the Creator, and Vishnu, the Protector, insisted that they were helpless. Finally, Shiva, the Destroyer, agreed. He would, he said, allow the Ganga to fall from the heavens onto his head, thus reducing the force of her descent.

The Ganga, prideful of her place in Heaven and always wilful in her ways, thought to sweep Shiva away with the sheer force of her descent. The god, sensing her intent, imprisoned her in his matted hair and held her captive until, moved by Bhagiratha's desperate pleas, he allowed her waters to trickle through his hair and flow down to earth.

Mythology thus neatly explains topography, weaving a story around the Ganga's origins in the Himalaya. To this day, it is believed, Shiva continues to hold the Ganga in his dreadlocks, controlling her force and allowing only a trickle to escape at a time. And thus, because of her contact with the Lord, she is ever pure, ever flowing, always divine.

The story goes that Bhagiratha rode ahead in a chariot pulled by the divine white elephant Airavata, hacking a way through the

Himalayan ranges for Ganga, who joyfully danced along in his wake. And thus they came, down the mountains and through the plains, bending south into the forests of Bengal, the river purifying everything in her path, until man and river reached Sagar Island and from there flowed into the netherworld, where her purifying touch restored the souls of the 60,000 sons of Sagara.

The day the Goddess descended to earth was Makar Sankranti, the day the sun passed from one constellation into another. And so, ever since then, on every Makar Sankranti – which falls in the middle of January – millions of devotees of all castes and creeds have gathered on that final teardrop-shaped island, Sagar, at a place called Gangasagar, to bathe in the holy waters.

Mythology often runs parallel to, and intertwines with, history. Thus, the spiritual importance of Bengal as the scene of Ganga's merger with the sea runs alongside the historical and commercial importance Bengal has always had for those who rule Delhi.

The Ganga, careening through 2,500 kilometres of India's soil and draining a quarter of her landmass, reaches the Bay of Bengal in several braided distributaries. These navigable distributaries allow the hinterlands to access the Bay and thus facilitate trade. Delhi was always invested in riches from lands near and far, and a good, deep port was therefore vital.

The small coastal town of Satgaon emerged as the trading linchpin of the thirteenth century. Strategically perched on the banks of the navigable Saraswati, at the cusp of the Bay of Bengal, it had access both inland and to the sea. Chinese dhows and junks anchored offshore, transferring their wares to smaller country boats that could ply deep into the interior, towards Sonargaon (near modern-day Narayanganj in Bangladesh), the then capital of southern Bengal.

Satgaon, the Moroccan traveler Ibn Battuta wrote, became 'a large town on the coast of the Great Sea,' a medieval-era marketplace for perfumes, for gold, for slaves of 'exquisite beauty'. Traders flocked to Satgaon, lured by the handsome profits to be had.[14]

The Saraswati river ruled the waterways for a few glorious centuries before it came to grief on account of an overlooked facet of Himalayan rivers and their capacity to carry vast quantities of silt down from the mountains. The Ganga carts more sediment than most rivers in the world – almost four times as much as the Amazon. This sediment fertilizes the delta and the plains, facilitating the growing of rice, millet, mustard, greens and fish – sustenance for the teeming millions of Bengal. But over time, the river chokes itself on its own silt – which is what happened to the Saraswati. Oceangoing vessels could no longer drop anchor at the port. Satgaon lost favour as the mouth to prosperity, while elsewhere a settlement along the Hooghly began to draw weavers and artisans and gained prominence.

In the seventeenth century, the British were steadily wresting control of Bengal from the Mughals. For them this new settlement – which they called Calcutta – became the port of choice. Job Charnock, an administrator with the East India Company, is credited with founding a trading port here in 1690.[15] For the emerging British Empire, the Hooghly was a gateway to Assam and a navigable waterway into the northern Gangetic plains.

Trade reoriented itself away from Asia and in the direction of Europe, supplying everything from gold and other precious metals to human currency in the form of indentured Indian labourers, who were shipped off to the far-flung reaches of the

British Empire. Calcutta on the east coast and Bombay on the west became the Empire's two most important Indian ports.

But the strong-willed Ganga had her own plans. Through the nineteenth century, the Hooghly was gradually silting up; by the early twentieth century, ships, wary of the massive underwater shoals that had formed, could barely reach the port of Calcutta. The importance of the port began to erode and with it the prosperity of the people of northern Bengal.

Under pressure from local merchants, the British passed the Calcutta Port Act of 1870, creating the Calcutta Port Commission, which attempted to dredge the river and clear it of obstacles. Defying these efforts, the Ganga continued to lay it on thick.

Arthur Thomas Cotton was a military engineer initially attached to the Madras administration. He was an outspoken proponent of engineering hydrology, of building dams and canals for irrigation, of using waterways rather than railways. In southern India, he led teams that constructed dams across the Kaveri river in what are now the districts of Thanjavur and Tiruchirapalli in modern-day Tamil Nadu; he then led similar projects on the Godavari and Krishna rivers.

In 1853 he turned his attention to Calcutta's growing woes. He suggested the construction of a dam across the Ganga at Farakka, in what is now the Murshidabad district of West Bengal. This, he theorized, would flush the Hooghly with the waters of the main channel of the Ganga and make it navigable again, thus reviving the dying port of Calcutta.

The British engineers, however, could not come to a consensus about a suitable site for the dam. The Cotton plan lay dormant for over a hundred years until 1957, when the government of newly independent India revived the idea as part of Prime Minister

Jawaharlal Nehru's quest to build 'temples to a new India'. They consulted British expert Dr W. Hensen, who ratified Cotton's choice of Farakka as a suitable site:

> The best and only technical solution of the problem is the construction of a barrage across Ganga at Farakka with which the upland discharge into the Bhagirathi-Hooghly can be regulated as planned, and with which the long-term deterioration in the Bhagirathi-Hooghly can be stopped and possibly converted into a gradual improvement. With a controlled upland discharge a prolongation of freshet period will be obtained, and the sudden freshet peaks which will cause heavy sand movement and bank erosion will be flattened.[16]

The project was now ratified by 'expert' imprimatur. Between 1963 and 1971, a 2.62-kilometre-long barrage was built at Farakka, with a feeder channel that pushed water into the Hooghly.

It did not work.

Hensen had not considered a key element – that the Hooghly was a tidal estuary. The river sees saline water inflows from the Bay of Bengal twice daily. The north-flowing tidal bore could be as much as 160 times than that of a south-flowing monsoon freshet. Given that, the amount of water washing upriver, carrying with it suspended sediment, was too much for the water from the Hooghly to push back out. The Farakka Barrage, thus, not only failed to accomplish its stated mission, but succeeded in creating a far more sinister problem.

Back in 2015, with Tarikul-bhai as my guide, I had made my first visit to the head of the Ganga delta, upstream of the Farakka Barrage. I made that visit and subsequent ones during the dry season, when the floodwaters had receded and the river flowed aquamarine and low.

Once the monsoon retreats, silt islands – called *chars* in West Bengal and *diaras* farther upstream in Bihar – rise out of the ebbing waters. These seasonal islands, formed by large deposits of silt during the dry months when the river's flow is lowest, defy the standard land/water binary. They are suspended particles, carted from elsewhere, carried in the womb of the river and birthed midstream, only to be claimed right back in subsequent seasons. These shifting sands are migrants in their own right and officially belong only to the river.

The silt islands are fertile, they yield bountiful crops; but they're too ephemeral for anyone to build long-term lives and livelihoods on. People who lose their land to the river 'recognize' it when the river births an island on the other side of the channel. Driven to desperation, these internally displaced people, these environmental migrants, take refuge on the chars. They mark out portions of the chars for themselves, give their portions names, till the land and plant their crops and reap their rewards until the onset of the next monsoon, when the surging river might take it all back, leaving them homeless and displaced, yet again.

And this is where the ill effects of the Farakka Barrage come into play. A river – especially a Himalayan river like the Ganga – is not simply a conduit for water. She carries with her much more by way of suspended particles and biota. She is a multitude unto herself.

By obstructing the natural course of the Ganga, the Barrage not only diverts water away but also blocks the transport of all that sediment. With nowhere to take the silt, the river dumps it at the dam. Over time these deposits accrete, raising the riverbed ever higher. This further checks the progress of the river. She then veers further left (since the right bank is rocky), carving new channels to get out of the trap. The veer is so severe now that she no longer flows coaxially to the barrage, but at an angle.

Her riverbed is so clogged now that, especially during the monsoon swells, she wanders all over the district of Malda. She is so off course that 'the river may outflank the barrage in the course of time, opening a new course through the Kalindri–Mahananda route,' says Rudra.

That malda in the eye of this man-made catastrophe is significant. For over four centuries, from the thirteenth century to the seventeenth century, the capital of Bengal was in the district now known as Malda. The cities known as Gaur, Pandua, Tanda and Rajmahal are all within a few kilometres of each other, at the head of the Ganga delta. Of these, Gaur was the city most favoured; it was the capital for all that time, with the exception of three decades or so.

In the early days Gaur was known as Lakhnawti, a Persian corruption of Lakshmanavati, the name given to the city during the reign of Lakshmanasena, the last ruler of the Sena dynasty. It was a thriving port on the Ganga, who flowed to the east, and the city was known for its fine muslin cloths and silks, prized the world over.

Gaur/Lakhnawti was a populous city,[17] with over 1.2 million families and an influx during festivals, as noted by the Portuguese traveller Manuel de Faria e Sousa in the mid-seventeenth century. 'Along the streets, which are wide and straight,' he writes, 'are rows of trees to shade the people, who are so very numerous that sometimes many are trod to death'. According to Sousa, in the 'principal city in Bengal' the boundaries were marked by high mud walls.

All that now remains of this fabled city, favoured by rulers such as the Mughal emperor Akbar, are the ruins of mosques and minarets, of high arching gateways and bridges. The monuments are all made of stone and brick, heavily inlayed and painted; many of the ruins still retain the original pigments, giving us an idea of how visually arresting the city might have been.

By the time the British surveyors came by in the eighteenth century, the city of Gaur had long fallen. The fact that the river appears on the eastern side of the city in early documentation but now flows quite a few miles to the west of it is proof enough that the migration of the river, sometime in the sixteenth century, likely played a major role in the city's decline.

Writing in 1915, Major F. C. Hirst, who was tasked with studying the problem of siltation along the Ganga, attributed the changes in the river's course to an earthquake in 1505. Probably measuring around 8.0 on the Richter scale, this was a major seismic event in the area. In the second half of the sixteenth century, the Ganga began to shift southward. Other rivers in the region also seem to have shifted course around this time.

As the Ganga migrated, the city of Gaur was likely left without a clean water supply, and the river's procession from east to southwest may have turned the region into a festering swamp. There was also a disastrous flood that engulfed the city, which may have contributed to its abandonment. In 1575, a plague reportedly created havoc throughout the city, which had been restored, but documentation from that era refers to Gaur as having 'inhospitable' and 'unhealthy' living conditions.

By the time Major James Rennell – who built a detailed atlas of Bengal and its various rivers – visited Gaur in 1760, it seemed to have been reclaimed by wilderness and was inhabited by deer, wild boar and even tigers that stalked the high grasses. A quarter of a century later, Henry Creighton surveyed the ruins of Gaur and in 1786 produced the only detailed work on the ancient city.

The main stem of the Ganga has held to its new course ever since. But the pileup of silt against the walls of the Farakka Barrage and the resulting rise in the riverbed is forcing the river into an oblique course, and it now threatens to return to the course it followed in the sixteenth century, farther east from where it flows today.

When the Ganga, foiled in its original course by the Farakka Barrage, swung wildly eastward into the channel she occupies today, she threw up a large sandbar, a char, just off the right bank. Over 300,000 homeless people from the lost villages on the left bank of West Bengal made a new home there, gave it a name and began to farm.

Palash Gachhi is like most chars: fertile, rich, unowned and open to anyone who wants to live on it. But it has a disconcerting subtext: When it first appeared, it was on the wrong side of the Jharkhand–West Bengal border, which unlike other state borders is not fixed. For some inexplicable reason, the Survey of India demarcated a part of the border between the two states as 'the path the Ganga takes'. The problem is that the Ganga adheres to no permanent path. She moves, she veers around obstacles – and the border moves with her.

Neither state likes the idea; both dispute the border. Jharkhand claims this char (which has over time added more sediment and joined the mainland) as its own, but it disowns the people who live on it. As far as officialdom is concerned, the people of Palash Gachhi are Bengalis living in Jharkhand. They fall between bureaucratic cracks: they can avail of no services from Jharkhand since the state does not recognize them as its people, nor can they avail themselves of services from West Bengal since they are technically living in Jharkhand. They are the nowhere people – nowhere on any government's radar, living in the here and now, unsure of what tomorrow holds.

Over a dozen of these disenfranchised people walk with us as we transect the char, discussing the issues they battle with. A transformer has been stolen, plunging one half of the meagrely electrified island into inky blackness. There is no sanitation; there is no light. There is a hospital building but there are no doctors; there are school buildings but no teachers. One school is exceptional in that it boasts a teacher – who shows up once every two days, teaches for a couple of hours, and leaves.

Given the lack of adequate health care, childbirth is a hazardous process, but there are an astounding number of little children on the char. It is a source of local pride. 'Have you seen so many kids anywhere else?' they ask.

The kids flock around us in dozens, bright-faced and eager-eyed. Reena, twelve, says she wants to become a teacher. Gehul, fourteen, wants to be a *moulvi*, a Muslim cleric. But they are the exceptions – children who have some notional idea of a 'future'. Most others just return blank stares when I ask what they want to do when they grow up.

A flock of women, their faces half-covered with their saris, accompany us, shepherding the children along. Rabha Bibi speaks up from among the throng. She lost her daughter at birth, she says ruefully, because she couldn't reach the hospital in time. When she went into labour, four men carried her on a *khatiya* (a woven cot), some three kilometres to the ghat. There they transferred to a country boat, which chugged along for almost an hour to reach the village of Panchanandapur. Then the men carried her another four kilometres to the only hospital the people of Palash Gachhi have access to. The journey took five hours – and in the end, it was all too late.

Rabha's story plays out in a generational loop. Her daughter has lost a child. Her neighbour has lost a friend, a woman who died in childbirth.

Since these nowhere people don't exist on paper, no statistical surveys have been done, no data mapped. But anecdotal evidence supports the belief that infant mortality and maternal mortality on these chars are inordinately high, as most births occur at home with no proper medical assistance. 'We need a functioning hospital here, to save the lives of children and mothers,' Rabha says to a crowd agreeing emphatically.

They hope, they dream, that life will change – but there is no indication that it ever will. And while the women continue to dream, their men take destiny into their own hands and go looking for jobs elsewhere. Some of these migrants are as young as twelve. The young girls, meanwhile, are enrolled in schools that aren't open, or that they're unable to attend because they have to earn money for their families.

'Erosion doesn't stop at our doorstep,' says Tarikul-bhai. 'It gnaws its way in, eating through every family.'

The able-bodied men leave; the women and children are left

behind in desperately degraded landscapes. There is no livelihood here, what with the fields, orchards, homesteads, schools, hospitals all taken by the impeded river.

On each visit over the years, I have seen groups of women and young girls hunched over baskets, rolling *beedis*. These are mini-cigars: tobacco rolled in the leaves of the tendu tree (*Diospyros melanoxylon*) and tied with a thread at one end.

I met a woman downstream of the barrage where the river, deprived of silt, tries to regain sediment load by gulping land. 'I know beedis are unhealthy,' she told me, her hands joined together in a plea. 'I know the UN is trying to get them banned. But if anything like that happens, what measly income we make will also stop.' Rolling a thousand beedis takes two days and fetches one hundred rupees – less than a dollar a day. If the beedis the women make are surplus to demand, they are not paid.

Anita Das, who lives upstream of the barrage and has lost everything for the first time, says beedi-rolling is the only option; there are no other jobs available. She has a high school certificate and is sharp as a tack, with a personality and aptitude that would likely fit on a corporate ladder – but such an option is not open to her ilk.

Following the loss of their home, Anita and her family of four live under a blue tarpaulin sheet, just like a hundred thousand others. 'You have no idea how hot it gets under there,' she says. 'Children have gotten sunburnt. Women have no privacy to change clothes. There are no bathrooms for us – we slink out at nights or in the early morning and walk long distances just to find an area private enough that we can use it for our ablutions.' She drops her eyes as she realizes that she is saying all this in front of the many men who have gathered around us.

We get up and head towards the edge of the chewed-up bank. She pushes the bicycle she rode on to meet us, talking continuously as we walk. She tells of desperate families marrying off their underage children – especially girls – since they are unable to support them; and how young boys are pressed into child labour – every paisa is invaluable when you have nothing, and no prospects. These children usually end up working in brick kilns, which not only employ underage children but also gouge the riverbank for clay, further weakening its structure.

On each visit, I meet more displaced people living in abject misery. On this latest trip, I talk with folks who have been 'rehabilitated' by the government and given *patta* (sanctioned land) for a 400-square-foot bamboo hut. Even as we're chatting, a man approaches me with a xeroxed sheet of faint lettering, clearly an official document attested by the District Commissioner's office.

He claims that the land these internally displaced people were given was his. He has the papers to prove it, he says. The government designated the riverine tract as a 'wasteland', which means that it can be allotted for 'better use'.

'My family has been farming on these lands, and these mango orchards have been in our family, for centuries,' he says, eyes flashing anger. 'How can the government just [designate] it as a wasteland and give it to them?'

Such disputes, I learned, were just one more consequence of a disrupted river, of an unclear border between states, of government departments at loggerheads, of sandbars that appeared and disappeared at the whim of the Ganga and of a people constantly uprooted through no fault of their own.

Inamul Haque and Tarikul-bhai, along with a few others, formed a committee back in 1995 to serve as a fulcrum for erosion-affected people. Their demands were simple then and are the same today: they ask that the government release information on vulnerable areas, acquire that land, pay the villagers at market rates and rehabilitate them in a fair and equitable manner.

They don't want the government to 'sanction relief', as they know from experience that it will be siphoned off by middlemen and functionaries who grow fat on the misfortune of their fellows. They would rather the government acquire the land at risk and in return give them new land, electricity, schools, hospitals and a livelihood away from the erosion.

The government has, instead, pumped tens of millions of rupees into fortifying the banks with boulders in a bid to stem erosion. It costs over 100,000 rupees to protect one metre of riverbank – and it doesn't guarantee against erosion, say experts, who point out that the river in spate washes the boulders away along with the land and everything on it. Yet the effort continues; overall, the government has spent upwards of 130 million rupees (about $1.6 million) on futile fortifications, as of 2015. That number is likely much higher now.

'It is a collusion between the government, which allocates the funds, and the contractors,' says Tarikul-bhai with the fatalistic smile of one who has seen it all before and is not fooled by promises anymore but has not lost hope. 'Often, they do 10 per cent of the work and claim [compensation] for 100 per cent. Also, they start work in the monsoons, which is stupid. How can you work on fortifying the bank when the soil is already wet and soft with rain?'

I look around me, at the gaunt, haunted faces of people who have lost everything; at the simmering anger of the man who claims the land the displaced people have been given is rightfully his; at Tarikul-bhai, who has been fighting for over three decades now for fair rehabilitation and who knows the fight has just begun.

We stand, all of us, just a hundred metres from the edge of an impeded river that has already gulped down nearly five hundred metres of land this season alone.

Before we get on the boat to return to Panchanandapur, Tarikul-bhai steps into a mosque to offer midday prayers.

The mosque hangs precariously over the bank. Its foundation has been sandbagged, and the swollen river laps persistently at it. Three children race each other up and down the cliffside, unmindful of a Gangetic river dolphin that arcs in and out of the river, soundlessly. Suddenly it hunts, and fish dart out of the water in desperation. A few seconds later, all is calm again – the fish relax until the next chase.

I climb down the gouged-out cliff and sit in the boat. As the boat bobs on a deceptively calm Ganga, my mind floats up several images: the Anthropocene interventions in the delta, including canals diverting waters from the main stems of rivers; extensive embankments that impede the transfer of silt carried by the river, thus suffocating the river and denying the delta of the valuable material; dams – from the high Tehri on the Alakananda in Uttarakhand to the Farakka here in Bengal – which have so altered the flows of the Ganga; and the consequences of this wilful mismanagement, borne by some of the most marginalized sections of society.

And yet, all along the Ganga in Bengal and along the Hooghly (which is also called the Bhagirathi here) are massive temples and holy places, some among the holiest in India – like the Kalighat just south of Kolkata.

Perhaps nowhere is this dichotomy more apparent than in the 2017 High Court decision in the state of Uttarakhand that declared the Ganga and her major tributary Yamuna to be rights-bearing 'living entities', and that defiling the rivers would be against the law.

The Supreme Court, however, overturned the High Court's ruling.[18] The apex court said, in effect, that if the Ganga and the Yamuna were people with rights, then pumping waste and sewage into them would amount to violating their right to life as outlined in Article 21 of the Constitution. This would make millions of households, industries and even pilgrims bathing in the rivers culpable. How would one adjudicate such potential prosecutions?

Explicit in the apex court's judgment is the fact that while on one hand we revere the Ganga as a Goddess, as a person, on the other, we continue to defile, impede, divert and suffocate her – and there is no redress.

Tarikul-bhai emerges from the mosque, his head still covered. We push off just as the sky begins to darken. All along the riverbank, life plugs on. A mother sits at the river's edge combing her daughter's long black hair, holding a pink hair-tie in her teeth. Four youth idle with fishing poles on the half-submerged roof that once belonged to a school. Further on, the jute cutters are still at it, thrashing and stripping the fibre and hanging it out to dry.

I am silent for the hour-long boat ride back. How can it be that a river is both sacred and profane at once? What will it take for us to make this right? I shake my head involuntarily. As if reading my mind, Tarikul-bhai says in Bengali, 'You cannot wake someone who only pretends to be asleep.'

A FLEETING FLASH OF FIN

IN A VILLAGE BY THE GANGA LIVED TWO YOUNG GIRLS WHO WERE firm friends. One tended gardens – she was a *maali*. The other was an oil seller, a *teli*. One morning, they set out to the river to bathe and fetch water. They began to argue about some little thing but, as arguments often do, this one too soon got out of hand. In their anger, they cursed each other, and no sooner had the words left their lips than each was transformed. The gardener became a *gharial* and swam away. The oil seller became a *bhulan* and dived deep into the river. Legend has it that this is how two of the most iconic denizens of the Ganga river system were born – the fish-eating crocodilian with a bulge at the end of its snout and the long-lipped Gangetic river dolphin, the apex predator of the river.[1]

In 2013, Paul Salopek set out on a 24,000-mile experiment in slow journalism. His mission: to walk in the footsteps of the first humans who migrated out of Africa in the Stone Age, a journey that began in Ethiopia and will end, in due course, at Tierra del Feugo at the extreme tip of Latin America. In February 2018, Paul crossed over from Pakistan into India at the Wagah border, and I joined him as his walking partner through Punjab and Rajasthan.

The walk is intense, and physically demanding – roughly thirty-five kilometres in the heat of an Indian summer, every single day. A hundred kilometres into India, at the Harike wetlands bordering the Tarn Taran Sahib district of Punjab, he catches a nasty bug. We decide to park for a few days. The break comes as a relief, and offers me a chance to catch up on my research on the region.

Harike falls under the Ramsar Convention on Wetlands of International Importance, established under the Ramsar Treaty of 1971 for the conservation and protection of wetlands. Wetlands are among the most diverse and productive ecosystems in the world, and excellent carbon sinks. This treaty defines wetlands to include lakes, rivers, marshes, bogs, peatlands, wet grasslands, underground aquifers, coral reefs as well as human-made sites like paddy fields and reservoirs. As I read up about the largest wetland in northern India, a line catches my eye: Indus river dolphins, that had 'gone extinct in India in the 1930s', had been 'discovered' again in the Beas river in 2007.[2]

That there are Indus dolphins in India is news to me. They are an endangered species, the once-teeming population now fragmented in short stretches of the main stem of the Indus river in Pakistan. The prospect of a sighting is tantalizing. I leave Paul to his rest and drive to the banks of the Beas and into the conservation area.

A low-slung boat slices across the river. A turbaned boatman stands tall at the prow; two farmers crouch between huge stacks of *sarkanda*, one of a few types of grass that cover the islands in the river. The water is dotted with sandbars, flanked on one bank by strands of high grass of the saccharum species and, on the other, by verdant fields of wheat. A man, ears plugged with loud thumping music and thus deaf to the world outside, waits at the edge of the river by the wheat fields, backpacking a translucent canister filled with a tangerine-coloured liquid. The lettering on it reads: 'WARNING: Don't spray at people and animals'.

I watch as he walks into the field that runs right up to the jagged line of the riverbank, and promptly starts the motor with a deafening put-put-put. He zigs and zags through the wheat field, painting the stalks, and occasionally the river, with the chemical.

'Have you seen the *bhulan* here?' I call out over the din, as the boat nears the bank. Bhulan, meaning 'long-lipped', is the local name for the snouted freshwater dolphin. Amarjeet Singh, the turbaned boatman, is an ex-army man who now plies a boat between the two banks. He points upstream. 'I saw two swim that way in the morning.'

I ask if we can go look for them.[3] He gives me a quizzical stare. Visitors are rare in this region. 'Sure,' he says, 'if you don't mind me ferrying people across while we do that.' I clamber onto the boat, and Amardeep swings it out in a wide arc around a reed island, pointing the prow at a smooth swathe of deep river.

The Indus dolphin is one of two subspecies of freshwater dolphins found in the Indian subcontinent. The other, the Gangetic dolphin, is native to the Ganga–Brahmaputra–Meghna river basin further east. Both varieties are blind. Thanks to millions of years spent in silty Himalayan meltwaters, the lens of the dolphin's eye has lost the ability to see, and it is able only to discern the direction of light. It navigates, finds food and identifies mates by echolocation. Both varieties swim on their side, hunt fish and live in human-dominated river systems. They are the top predators in a river, and highly endangered.

Colonial records suggest that the Beas river teemed with life in the nineteenth century. 'The Beas abounds with cyprinus roe, a species of carp, good for eating; also with a species of silurus about the size of a large trout, but very ugly, like a tadpole, and eaten by the natives only; also with tortoises and porpoises and alligators. Some officers the other day went out fishing and are said to have caught more than 1,900 fish,' mentioned James Coley in his *Journal Sutlej Campaign Of 1845–6*. Coley's 'alligators' were likely gharials, and the 'porpoises' Indus dolphins.

In 1878, the Scottish zoologist John Anderson, the first to describe the Indus dolphin, noted that river dolphins swam the length of the Indus basin from the delta to the foothills of the Himalaya, across what is now India and Pakistan. He also put down the Gangetic dolphin's range as the entirety of the Ganga–Brahmaputra basin.

In the second half of the twentieth century came the barrages and the dams, as the newly independent nation pushed forth its development mission. By 1971, twenty dams and barrages punctuated the Indus and its main tributaries, chopping up the dolphin's range into seventeen sections. By the 1990s, this fragmentation had slashed the dolphin's range by 80 per cent.

Today the Indus dolphin is found in only five of sixteen sections of the Indus in Pakistan. In India, it is found only in this one section of the Beas, a stretch bookended by the Pong dam in Himachal Pradesh and the Harike barrage at the confluence of the Beas and the Sutlej.

The Sutlej, in this region, flows doom-black and looks nothing like its mellower counterpart, which is a light tan. The two rivers join to continue as the Sutlej, into Pakistan. If, that is, the Sutlej below the Harike barrage has any 'flow' at all – it is more sand than water. Along this length, the Sutlej is bloated with the gunk that the tanneries in Jalandhar, Ludhiana and other upstream towns pump into it. This ghastly mix of rotting leather and assorted chemicals generates a noxious stench that hangs over the area like a physical presence, numbing the senses. At its fount, the Sutlej is classified as 'A', fit to drink; this far down, however, it has degraded to 'D' and, in some places even 'E', which is as awful as it gets on the pollution scale.

The stretch of river Amarjeet pilots us through is part of the Beas Conservation Area, and it looks and smells clean. Grass and sedge-covered river islands, mercifully free of plastic trash, teem with bird life: prinias, skimmers, terns, visiting Siberian gulls, plovers, stilts, pied kingfishers, red-wattled lapwings, Eurasian coots, little grebes and majestic grey and purple herons.

Dr Gitanjali Kanwar, World Wildlife Fund India's coordinator for rivers, wetlands and water policy, leads a project to repopulate the gharial in this stretch of the Beas, in an attempt to mitigate the 80-plus per cent drop in population in the last decade. The reptiles introduced into the Beas as part of the project were juveniles; it will take them a few years to reach breeding age. Once they mature, the female will lay her eggs in the sandbars that stripe this silty river. For now, though, they are not yet strong enough to swim against the current and risk being swept down towards the barrage. Dr Kanwar and her team do daily transects along the river to make sure the gharials are safe.

Judging by how far Amarjeet has to push his oar to hit bottom, we are now in water that is a few metres deep – dolphin territory, for the cetacean likes extensive pools of water.

It is not easy to spot river dolphins. Unlike their photogenic marine cousins, they do not jump and spin and frolic. The passage of a river dolphin has a blink-and-miss-it quality – its finned back arcs out of the water and then slides into it in a flash. Like the best of Olympic divers, they leave no telltale splash behind; a dolphin could well have surfaced beside or behind you, and then vanished just as quickly while you were scanning the waters ahead.

The melodic *kirtan* of the evening prayer from the village gurudwara drifts across the still waters. I keep my eyes fixed on the stretch of water ahead while Amarjeet scans the river behind us and to the sides. 'There!' He yells from behind. I whirl around. Too late – there is only a ripple to show where a dolphin had surfaced seconds earlier.

Like the Iñupiaq 'qala' or a 'slick of flat water' that follows the submergence of a whale, an oval hush of ripples is the signature of the river dolphin.

I count down ninety seconds, the average time a river dolphin – a mammal that has to surface for air – stays underwater before coming up for a breath. Three … two … one … and on cue, not twenty yards away, a curved grey-brown snout breaks the surface, pointing at the sky, teeth gleaming white through its trademark 'smile'.

The dolphin disappears underwater and, another ninety seconds later, resurfaces – this time, with a youngster in tow. She is a mother! For the better part of an hour, the dolphin and her calf arc in and out of the water, sometimes barely surfacing. There are no other boats around, no gawking tourists, no cannonades of clicking cameras. Just us – and two of South Asia's rarest river dolphins, dipping and diving with abandon.

The experience is addictive. I return the next day, and the day after that. And my luck holds – at some points the mother and her calf show up, at other times a lone male. On occasion, he is accompanied by another juvenile male. At times I am on a boat; at others I trail my legs over the edge of the riverbank and watch.

On my fourth morning by the river, Amarjeet looks grave. 'The river levels are dropping,' he says, pointing upstream. 'They are not releasing water.' This is the beginning of summer; the previous monsoon has not been sufficient, and snowfall too has been scant. Farms, towns, villages along the Beas are thirsty; water is being held back and redirected to meet their needs and, as a consequence, this stretch is running low.

A desiccating river is the death knell for dolphins, who love the deep and need at least a couple of metres of water to thrive. Low dry-season discharge in rivers, due to upstream diversions and impoundment by dams, is the main reason for the declining range of the Indus dolphin. When river levels fall, dolphins head for the deepest parts, where fish abound. But so do the fishermen accidentally snaring dolphins in their nets. The result is death.

Local boatmen tell me some weeks later that water levels had fallen by several feet more. A newspaper article echoed their alarm: 'Beas river going dry, aquatic life in danger'.[4]

These issues are not peculiar to the Beas or the Indus. In the summer of 2016, I had witnessed historically low levels in the Ganga, where the other South Asian cetacean – the Gangetic dolphin – lives.

Eastern Bihar's Bhagalpur district, a sixty-seven-kilometre stretch of the Ganga, between the towns of Sultanganj and Kahalgaon, is home to the Vikramshila Gangetic Dolphin Sanctuary, the only reserve legally dedicated to India's national aquatic animal, the Gangetic dolphin.

With me is Nachiket Kelkar, a soft-spoken researcher in his thirties, affiliated at this time to the Ashoka Trust for Research in Ecology and Environment, and Subhasis Dey, a spirited, deeply empathetic researcher with the Vikramshila Biodiversity Research and Education Centre. Having worked with river communities for over a decade, their knowledge of the ecology of river dolphins and fisheries is encyclopaedic.

We are on the Ganga, searching for dolphins in the sanctuary. As we coast along, a row of toddy palms come into view on the distant south bank. Two decades ago, the river lapped at those palms; today the waterline is about half a kilometre away. It's our first visual marker of the extent to which the flows in the Ganga have reduced; this year, the depth sensor tells us that it's at an all-time low.

Tear-shaped silt islands or *diaras*, dotted with clumps of sedge, grass and local vegetation, rise from the water. These temporary islands that emerge from the river are creature-havens. Two bright-beaked skimmers perch on one edge; lesser whistling teals brown an opposite edge; open-billed storks forage in the shallows; a row of hard-shelled tent turtles basking in the sun plop back hurriedly into the river, alarmed by the put-put of our outboard motor.

Walls of silt rise up from the green waters on both sides of the river, pocked, like ancient computer punch cards, with the homes of bank-mynas. The birds flit in and out, dipping and rising in a murmuration. A greater adjutant stork wades past, its wizened face wary as it examines us. Two more display their massive black-and-white wingspans further out on the diara, and a fourth makes an awkward landing. This part of eastern Bihar is one of only three regions where these endangered storks breed. There is, reportedly, a stable population of around 300 here.

All along the Ganga–Brahmaputra–Meghna basin, silt islands that are neither land nor water go by different names: they are called diaras in Bihar, chars in West Bengal and *chaporis* in Assam. All of them are transient, thrown up and reclaimed at will by the river, yet all coveted and claimed by opportunistic riverine folk who farm and fish and hunt on them. Silt transforms floodplains into food bowls and is vital in delta-making.

Tumbling down from the Gangotri glacier some 1,600 kilometres to the northwest, in the Uttarakhand Himalaya, the Ganga begins its descent as Bhagirathi. Folding the Alakananda river into itself at Devprayag, the now-swollen river cleaves the Himalayan mountains, picking up massive amounts of silt along the way, and hurtles down towards the plains. Its white waters roil past Rishikesh, grow calmer at Haridwar, and flow southeast to the floodplains of Uttar Pradesh.

The river turns putrid at Kanpur owing to the toxic inflow from local tanneries, and the water is so severely extracted that it is almost nothing but sand when it flows into Allahabad. Here the Chambal joins the Ganga, its waters replenishing the flow. At Varanasi, millions of worshippers dunk their sins in the river and supposedly emerge cleansed – and the river flows on, its waters now dark with foul foam, fecal matter, chemicals and floating cadavers.

And then the Ganga enters Bihar. After having suffered the conurbations of civilization and religion alike, the river here is renewed by the waters of the Ghagra, Gandak and Kosi rivers which flow down from the Nepal Himalaya. In Bihar, it is no longer the 'holy waters of Gangotri' but the sum of its tributaries, and that is its saviour. It now meanders, braiding its way through the floodplains for another thousand kilometres down to West Bengal and Bangladesh, en route to its home in the Bay of Bengal.

Nachiket, Subhasis and I intercept the river in the lower floodplains. Its swatch here is arced with oxbows and punctuated with comma-shaped diaras. From the lower observation deck of this boat, specially outfitted for dolphin surveys, three pairs of eyes – two experienced, one novice – seek signs of the trademark arc of soft grey, of a beak-like snout cleaving the surface to breathe, of the gentle curve of dorsal fin diving back in. We had spotted one dolphin when we pushed away from shore, but have glimpsed none since. This, my researcher friends point out, is unusual; in this season, seventy to a hundred dolphin sightings are par for this short course.

We drift past the four-kilometre-long Vikramshila bridge at Bhagalpur, and past the burning ghat. The Bhagalpur Engineering College hostel comes into sight – the outer limit of safe passage along the river. Beyond this, men on horseback roam the diaras with guns and black flags, waylaying boats, looting and, occasionally, even killing those who refuse to comply with their demands.

We turn around and return to the Sultanganj ghat, having traversed a stretch where fifteen to twenty individual dolphins have hung around for years. Now, barring the solitary early sighting, there are none to be seen.

In March 2016, the government of India passed the National Waterways Act (NWA), which identified 106 rivers that will be engineered into cargo-carrying waterways. Shipping is 'greener' than road traffic, goes the rationale. But, says Nachiket, there has been no discussion, in administrative and political circles or even among environmental and scientific groups, on the importance of riverine ecology and of the lives and livelihoods it sustains.

As per the plan, National Waterway 1 (NW1) will run from Haldia in West Bengal to Allahabad in Uttar Pradesh along the Hooghly, Bhagirathi and Ganga. It will involve the construction of more barrages along the river and heavy dredging of silt, so that a width of forty-five metres and a depth of three metres can be maintained throughout to enable passage for barges carrying 1,500–2,000 tonnes of cargo.

'Constructing more dams between Allahabad and Haldia will convert the Ganga into big ponds,' Bihar's chief minister Nitish Kumar said in 2015. 'It will adversely affect the river's ecosystem. We should allow uninterrupted flow of the Ganga waters.'

Nachiket has called out the implications of the NWA. Now, as we sit by the Ganga watching the sun haemorrhage into the river, his observations come alive. We see a dredger silhouetted against the fiery orange shimmer of the water. It scoops up sediment from the riverbed and plumes it back into the main channel of the river. This is crucial to maintaining the NW1's navigability, given the heavy sediment load the Ganga carries. But it can also spell the end for various aquatic species.

Many kinds of fish live, feed and breed at the bottom of the riverbed and under small rocks. Dredging disrupts and scoops out these breeding and feeding grounds endangering the survival of the species, Nachiket explains, as we sip chai by the river's edge one squally May evening in 2016.

The Gangetic dolphin, like its Indus counterpart, is almost completely blind. Sound to it is everything. It navigates, feeds, mates, breeds, nurses babies and circumvents danger by echolocation: dolphins send out sound waves that bounce back, allowing them to sense where something is located. The hellish sounds of dredgers and the engines of cargo-carrying vessels disrupt the dolphins' ability to hear lower echolocation frequencies, which makes it severely difficult for them to find food and to navigate. Not to mention that the physical upheaval of river sediment caused by dredging is also disruptive for river dolphins.

Gangetic dolphins come up to take in lungfuls of air roughly every two minutes. Intensive dredging operations seem to increase this time threefold, a clear physiological stress response. Moreover, these dolphins are 'highly vocal in normal circumstances' but tend to be far quieter on dredging days than they are otherwise. The Gangetic dolphins also die from propeller hits, while tourist cruise ship noises suppress their dive times.

As if this list of adversities wasn't long enough already, increased shipping traffic along these rivers also brings with it the likelihood of catastrophic mishaps. In the first seven months of 2020 alone, one river – the Hooghly in West Bengal – saw eight ships carrying fly ash capsize, spilling their toxic loads into the river and contaminating it for its own denizens as well as all those people whose livelihoods depend on it.

The estimated number of Gangetic dolphins in all of South Asia is under 2,000. A similar number of Indus dolphins has been counted in Pakistan, besides a handful in India. The Ganga–Brahmaputra–Meghna river basin and the Indus river basin are their natural homes. Both river systems are now fragmented by dams, scoured by dredgers, polluted by effluents and sewage, and roiled by shipping.

On 15 August 2020, the prime minister of India marked the seventy-third anniversary of India's independence by announcing Project Dolphin, aimed at protecting both sub-species. The plan is to provide alternate livelihoods to fishermen, put in place anti-poaching activities and curb pollution. One wonders why the project indirectly places blame on the fishermen for endangering dolphins. I think to myself how the plan stops short of naming, let alone addressing, the serious issues of impounded water with diminishing river flows and disastrous waterways.

A country that constantly aspires to and compares itself with China's development might do well to consider the fate of the *baiji*[5], a species of freshwater dolphin once hailed as the 'goddess of the Yangtze'. As China industrialized and made heavy use of the river for hydroelectricity and transport, baiji population declined dramatically. In 2001, the Chinese government announced a conservation plan to protect the Yangtze dolphin, but a surveillance expedition in 2006 found no trace of the cetacean. The baiji is now believed to be the first dolphin species driven to extinction. Unless India changes course with respect to its interrupting and diverting rivers, its shipping lanes and dams, it may be just a matter of time before the India's National Aquatic Animal suffers a similar fate.

I sit one afternoon on the banks of the Beas, dangling my legs over the edge. An Indus dolphin mother arcs in and out, followed by its calf, and I wonder, *do we even understand what it means when we wilfully snuff out a species?*

Aldo Leopold's story in *A Sand County Almanac* rushes unbidden into my mind: One afternoon a group of young foresters in southwestern US sit down on a rimrock for lunch. Far below them, a pack of wolves begins to ford a river. Filled with the trigger-itch, the men shoot down at the wolves, bullets ricocheting off the cliff walls. The thinking at the time was that less wolves meant more deer and more deer meant happy hunters. They bring down a wolf.

Among these foresters is a young Aldo Leopold. Decades later, when he becomes an ecologist, he recalls the moment. 'We reached the old wolf in time to watch a fierce green fire dying in her eyes. I realized then, and have known ever since, that there was something new to me in those eyes - something known only to her and to the mountain'. With no predators, the deer would chew up the landscape until it is over-browsed and devastated. Eventually, all the mountainsides would go brown. The rains then would wash away the slopes, leaving only dustbowls. Leopold would write three decades later, 'Perhaps this is the hidden meaning in the howl of the wolf, long known among mountains, but seldom perceived among men.'

As I watch, the older dolphin's grey fin barely breaks the surface, and seconds later a small snout pokes through the tea-soup-coloured river. I cannot help but feel that these ancient rivers and cetaceans understand their interconnected web far better than we ever will.

HUNTING WITH DOLPHINS

IT IS THE FINAL WEEK OF FEBRUARY 2017, THE LAST OF THE dark nights in the hunting season on the Brahmaputra. The sun is down, leaving behind a rose-pink sky that fades to purple, then indigo which ultimately turns an inky black. We can't see a thing. Not the horizon, nor the moon, the stars, not even a hand held in front of our faces. It is as if the world were doused in Japanese ink.

My friend and I are inching up the massive river with two fishermen, Lekhu and Ranjan, in their long, low-slung dinghy. It is the dry season; the river's shallow course here is braided with sandy shoals.

Lekhu and Ranjan are among the last of their tribe in Assam – handheld harpoon fishermen who fish on the blackest nights of the dry season, when the river runs clear and low. What makes them special is that they fish alongside the Gangetic dolphins.

Now the boat bumps up against something and runs aground. We step onto a silt island – a chapori. It is neither land nor water, neither predictable nor permanent. It rises as the silt piles up and submerges as the river current erodes it, carrying the silt away; it gives, it takes back.

These fertile chaporis come in varying degrees of robustness, depending on the amount of silt accreted and the vegetation anchoring the outcropping to the bed. Adventurous risk-takers settle on the larger, more robust ones. A chapori belongs to no government or individual; it exists on no map. Google, in fact, tells us we are in the middle of the main stem of the Brahmaputra. The chapori we are on will, in all likelihood, disappear in a few months, as the river swells during the next monsoon.

Flashlights clamped in our mouths, we juggle ropes and stakes out of the boat and pitch our tents. The fishermen start a cooking fire, and against its light, our shadows dance on the river. Dinner is rice – lots of it – and potatoes in a tomato curry. As we eat, the river gurgles softly near us and the wind brings the sound of drumbeats. The world's largest river island, Majuli, home to Vishnu-worshipping monks, is not far off. 'We will set out at 9 p.m., after dinner,' says Lekhu, the senior of the two fishermen. 'It will be cold; wear something warm.'

The men fill a kettle-shaped lamp with kerosene and poke a wick into its spout. With clay collected from the riverbank, they fix the lamp onto the front of the boat, just beneath the prow. A wind starts up as a whisper that soon turns into a howl, raising small waves that lap furiously at the sandbank. The fire goes out; flying sand enters our tents, stinging our faces. High wind means no fishing, Lekhu warns us.

At 9 p.m., the wind is still fierce. We wait. An hour or so later, it relents. Lekhu lights the lamp on the boat. We clamber onboard and push off from the sandbar. Lekhu stands tall at the prow, a six-pronged harpoon in hand, while Ranjan perches aft and navigates with the oar. The two of us crouch between them, in single file. We can see only a small arc in front of the boat by the lamp's light, which glows orange and burns heavy, leaving a trail of smoke in our wake.

Lekhu's eyes are fixed on that arc of light as he uses his harpoon to call the dolphins. He teases the water, moving the tip of the instrument in wide curves along the surface. Nothing happens. He spears the harpoon into the river, making sloshing sounds. Still nothing.

Ranjan guides the boat downstream, zigging from right bank to left and zagging around shoals. Lekhu dunks the harpoon in the water and raises it quickly, causing a soft plop. He agitates the water, sending ripples out wide, but to no avail. The two fishermen exchange comments in hushed voices. I gather that the season is drawing to a close.

Time passes, and then, out of the pitch black of the night, there is a whoooooosh off to our right. The flashlight beam lights up the dorsal fin of a Gangetic dolphin. As the first one disappears, another arcs out of the water, ghostly white in the glow. A mother and her calf have joined us.

I switch off my light and listen to the swoosh of their breath through the blowholes. They stay with us; Lekhu is alert now for signs of fish fleeing ahead of the dolphins. He harpoons one, then another. The impaled fish come up squealing and yapping.

The sounds surprise me at first. Then I remember Nachiket telling me about fish that make noises. Catfish, prawns, crabs and river puffers all make sounds, but this is the first time I've heard a fish squeal. It thrashes for a while at the bottom of the boat, fighting for air, and then falls silent.

'Fish are scarce,' Lekhu tells us. 'When there's plenty, the dolphins get excited. They come close enough to rock the boat and even slap its sides.' The dolphins today are just ten yards ahead of us. I put my camera down. We are bobbing and swaying in this thin, long boat on the mighty Brahmaputra, in total darkness and silence, with a river dolphin mum and calf for company. A shiver runs down my spine, and I hug myself and smile at the ghostly grey arcs beside us. If meeting an endangered wild creature in its space, with its offspring in tow, far away from any protected area was not in itself special, we are witnessing a human collaborating with a wild animal – a way of life that is also endangered.

I bowed my head and exhaled long and slow. Fish populations in the Brahmaputra have been dwindling, reports indicate, by as much as 80–85 per cent in some places. Many small species of indigenous fish, neither studied nor named, are likely lost forever. As no baseline study was ever conducted, there is not enough data to quantify this loss. All we have is the oral evidence of fishermen who live on these waters and tell tales of what once was.

Three years earlier in Upper Assam: winter has long vanished, leaving behind only a hint of nip in the fierce pink of the gloaming. The Subansiri river makes its way down from Tibet to join the Brahmaputra, flowing fat and placid across the plains. Orchid-swathed forests with clumps of fern rise black and feathery against a salmon sky. From the far bank, a boatman in a dugout ferries seven people across using a bamboo pole as an oar.

Trucks wheeze and grumble along raw roads of scree, carrying towering piles of smooth, round rock. The grey dust of their passing obscure small-scale factories pulverizing great quantities of rock into cement for dams, roads, buildings.

The light is fading fast. Professor Lakhi Hazarika, who teaches fish zoology at the local college in Lakhimpur, and I have jumped into our car at the urging of the driver in order to return to the town. This is 'elephant hour' and, in an area famous for 'angry rogue elephants at twilight', our driver is scared. The professor, a scientist, has no such apprehensions. As we crest a bridge over a stream, he motions for our driver to halt. Jumping out of the car, he runs down the bank. I follow suit.

We rush across the soft sand, past massive elephant footprints, to an area with a smudge of water. He crouches at its edge and carefully moves a small river rock. Two baleful eyes stare back at us – a snakehead fish, about as long as my index finger, heavy with eggs. 'This is an endangered species,' the professor explains.

Small indigenous fish like the snakehead find refuge around river rocks and fallen logs, in the nooks and crannies of soft-flowing streams, and in coves. These are prime habitats for the fish – they breed under the rocks and submerged logs, or near the roots of trees along the tiny streams that flow down from the eastern Himalayas. Those streams and rivers are now being mined for rocks and boulders, depriving the fish of their safe spaces. 'If you take those "obstacles" away, you destroy vital fish-breeding habitats.'

With the supply of small indigenous fish declining by 85–90 per cent over the past decade, fishermen are sliding into poverty. They cannot find enough fish in the river to sell, much less to eat. In the markets of Dibrugarh, 90 per cent of the fish consumed in the town is trucked in, on beds of ice, from farms in Andhra Pradesh, and this is true for most other cities on the banks of the mighty Brahmaputra that was once highly biodiverse.

The sociological and economic hit the river fisheries are taking is repeating itself all over the subcontinent.

A few months after my trip with Professor Hazarika, I walk through fishing villages along the Teesta in Bangladesh and see scarcity and hunger everywhere. India's barrage upstream impounds vital water, desiccating the lower riparian country in the dry season. It's not difficult to join the dots. No water, no fish. No fish, no money. No money, no food.

All along the Brahmaputra, wetlands serve as nurseries for fish. Brought in by the floods that spill over the banks and into the wetlands, the fingerlings find space to grow, awaiting the next flood to make their way back into the tributaries and from there into the main stem of the river.

The embankments erected to control floods, however, have cut the wetlands off from this main stem, adversely affecting the natural replenishment of fish stocks. With their livelihoods unsettled by the double whammy of upstream mining and disappearing wetlands, fishermen resort to unsustainable fishing methods that in turn accelerate the depletion of fish populations. Artisanal fishermen like Lekhu and Ranjan are being pushed to the brink.

We spend three hours on the river, fishing in the company of two sets of dolphins, but have only two fish to show for it. Returning to our camp well after midnight, we crawl into our tents. The night closes in on us, its silence punctuated only by the tympanic slap of water.

As dawn approaches, the tan-coloured chapori reveals itself. It is flat as a pancake; there is no chance for privacy during one's morning ablutions. Lekhu and Ranjan snore rhythmically inside their tent. I drag my drone's Pelican case to the edge of the sandbar, perch on it and scribble notes while the experience is still fresh.

A commotion erupts in the water right in front of me. A million bubbles burst from an eddy. Panicked fish fly into the air. The hump of a dorsal fin and a spray of misty water cue me in – a Gangetic dolphin is on the hunt. I watch, stunned by the cetacean's speed, grace and power, too rapt to even break out my camera. And then, as suddenly as it had started, the hunt is over, the fish have scattered and the dolphin moves away. The river settles back into its natural rhythms, the currents making soft sounds again as they churn the silty waters.

Lekhu starts a fire for the morning tea. He and Ranjan make plans to move camp further upstream in the hope of better fishing. We pack up and load the dinghy. As we row upstream, Lekhu lowers a fishing net into the water. A raucous flock of the endangered greater adjutant stork lifts off into the leaden skies. A melancholic song wafts from downriver; in the distance, we spot a lone fisherman in a boat.

Our fishermen guides know him; he is called 'the mad one' for his incessant singing. Lekhu hauls up his net with two fish in it, and we disembark on another chapori. This one is a sizeable strip with a jetty at the far end, and there are signs of human presence.

We gather around yet another cooking fire. The two freshly caught fish are on the menu. 'Seven or eight years ago, we'd make about 12,000 rupees in a week of hunting,' Lekhu says, as he fillets the fish. 'Now we hunt all five months of the dry season and still don't make that much.'

The rivers that feed the Brahmaputra are changing constantly, and there are rumours that the Brahmaputra itself will be turned into a national waterway. The wetlands, already under assault from all kinds of development, will be further stressed, and the fisherfolk – their lives and livelihoods – will suffer the cumulative impact's worst effect.

Not so long ago, fish markets along the banks of the Brahmaputra bustled with dozens of fish varieties. Now most of these shops are shuttered; the few that remain open sell those ice-box fish brought in from the fish farms of Andhra Pradesh, thousands of kilometres away.

Lekhu and Ranjan know that their special skill, hunting alongside dolphins, has reached its use-by date. They may not return next year. Lekhu has some knowledge of masonry; Ranjan will find some odd job.

The dolphin's fate, too, is uncertain.

Three years prior, in 2014, on a river to the southwest of Dhaka one monsoon day, we had been calling out to every fishing boat we encountered: 'Any fish? How many you got?' Usually, the answer was a shake of the head, a moan that floated over the waters: 'No fish. There are no fish in the river.' But once came this reply: 'Shushuk!' Dolphin. Caught in a net not cast for it.

This is one way dolphins die – especially the young ones. Either they go to feed on fish trapped in fishing nets or, worse, they swim right into nets strung across the width of a river. The nets weave themselves in and out of the white parabolic curve of the dolphins' sharp, clean teeth, snapping the snouts shut.

Adult dolphins are strong enough to cut through the mesh, but the babies, like the not-yet-eight-month-old 'shushu' this fisherman inadvertently caught, can do nothing. Unable to come up to breathe, they thrash wildly in the water, often entangling themselves further. Eventually, they suffocate and perish.

I remember touching the lifeless cetacean. Its skin had felt smooth, almost like the rubber of a scuba diver's outfit. It was cold too, with white chalk-like gashes on its back and fins – the marks of its fruitless struggle with the net. Its near-blind eyes were like tiny beads. I knew the theory – the silty waters of these rivers meant that they had adapted to the murkiness by relinquishing sight for a keen hearing, using echolocation to navigate. Their eyes could not see anything but, maybe, the direction of light. Even so, I was astonished by the tiny, clouded opening.

The fishermen, though, were going home hungry, their debts deepening with every drawing of an empty net.

Night falls quickly in northeast India. There is no wind to delay us. We set off from the chapori for the last hunt of the season. The blackness closes in on us; the only sound is that of Lekhu teasing the waters with his harpoon. Two dolphins materialize ahead of us, then another, followed by a mother and her calf.

They whoosh and arc and dip and sigh. There are no fish for them or us.

Whichever side of the net you are on, there is only loss.

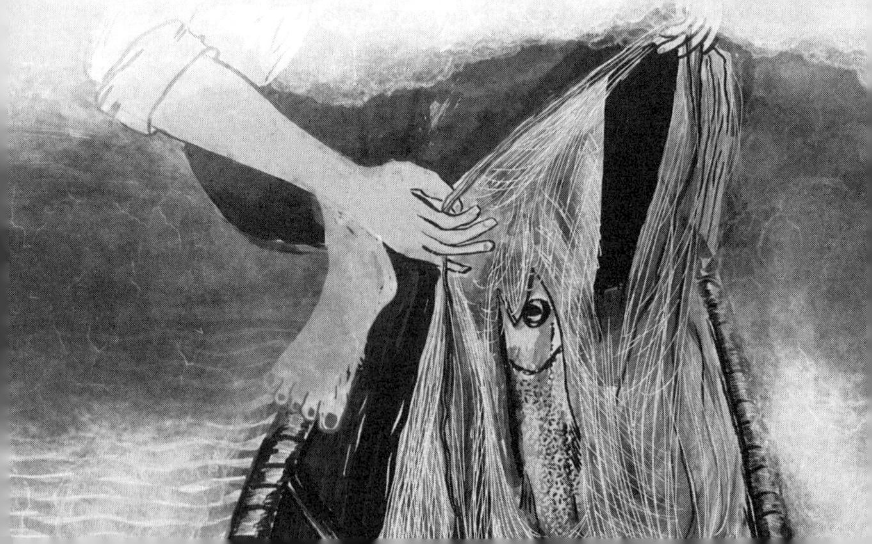

FADING TO BLACK

THE BRAHMAPUTRA IS A MOODY RIVER, TEMPESTUOUS AND WILFUL. The channels it flows through in the morning can become silt-laden and impassable by evening. Sandbars materialize where water had flowed just hours earlier. Silt piles up high; the river eddies around it, eroding the silt and carrying it along on its course to pile it up elsewhere, in an endless sequence of creation and destruction. What was deep the day before becomes shallow; what was shallow grows deep as the forever shifting silt alters the riverscape incessantly. Nothing is as it was, or as it will be. The Brahmaputra has a mind of its own.

A drone's eye view shows in the distance the cerulean ranges of the eastern Himalaya, their peaks obscured by gravid clouds that meld into a stone-grey sky. Thin white ribbons of water snake down the sides of the mountains in separate strands before braiding into larger ribbons that gain in heft and cascade down to the valley below. Through this valley rushes the Brahmaputra, a turgid band some eighteen kilometres wide.

Standing on a boat, in the middle of a swollen Brahmaputra during monsoons, one would be hard-pressed to see either bank. The river feels like a vast, endlessly eddying sea cloaked in a thick white fog.

It wasn't always like this.

On the night of 15 August 1950, the people of Assam – as elsewhere in India – were winding down their Independence Day celebrations when, at 7:39 p.m., the earth heaved with unimaginable violence.

The intrepid English botanist, explorer and author Frank Kingdon-Ward, who worked all over Tibet and also moonlighted as a spy for the British Empire, was in the village of Rima in Tibet, about 130 kilometres downstream, at the time of the earthquake. He noted that the main tremor lasted for a good five or six minutes: 'It was certainly of long duration and extreme violence,' he wrote, 'the motion being vertical, as though the crust of the earth were caving in, but found difficulty in getting through the hole.'

He recalls 'muffled booms', explosions that were heard 200 miles away in Burma; he writes of collapsed hillsides exposing ashen granite, and rivers that 'ran so thick with mud that the astonished fish found their world turning solid'.

Reports of 'millions of dead and dying fish' and 'a tide of tens of thousands of uprooted trees and the bodies of tigers, elephants, and other wild life', and a Brahmaputra 'blackened with sulphur … churned up from the earth's innards' speak to the devastation the 8.7-magnitude quake unleashed on an unsuspecting populace.

Tributaries, temporarily dammed by the initial landslides, broke free, and walls of water rising twelve feet high swept everything in its path. The voluminous debris – boulders from the collapsed hills, tons of mud, entire forests uprooted in an instant, the detritus of obliterated homes – was carried along by the surging waters of the Lohit, Dibang and Dihang rivers and deposited on the plains.

Clogged with this wreckage, the riverbed rose to heights of 0.5–3.5 metres over a 300-kilometre stretch. Channels in regular use became choked, as new ones opened up. The swollen river spilled over its banks, causing some of the worst flooding in the history of the region. Steamboats found themselves stranded on islands that had formed below their keels.[1]

As the churning waters carved new pathways, the river, originally around two kilometres wide, grew nine times, and even wider in some places. The Brahmaputra would never be the same again – triggered by the seismic upheaval, it had morphed into an organism deadly, unpredictable, untameable.

At Singhajan Ghat on the north bank of the Brahmaputra, Kalu Das, a spry man in his sixties squats low to the ground and points to a deep crack running parallel to the riverbank. 'See?' He skips ahead a few feet and points to another crack, then another some three feet away, and one more two feet further downstream.

The cracks, like the bite marks of some gigantic predator, are relics of the area where, on one monsoon night in 2015, the surging river swallowed a thirty-metre chunk of land. Areca nut trees and bamboo, shorn of their moorings, lay any old how in the river, their roots poking up like so many hands desperately clutching at a bank that is no longer there.

For locals such as Kalu Das, reading the cracks to predict which portion of the bank will go next has become an existential skill. 'I had to move my house there,' he says, pointing to a bamboo shack a few metres away where an older man, sat hunched over. A young mother and her toddler child stood nearby, gazing out over the turbulent river.

The water was over a kilometre away a few years ago, Kalu Das recalls. Semaphoring its intent one crack at a time, the river has eaten its way up to the doorsteps of these homes. During and after the monsoon season, the remorseless undercurrents slice away the bottom of the bare cliff. Land falls away in chunks, and new cracks open further inland. The residents of the ghat read the cracks, try to calculate which section of land the river will swallow next, and shift their cottages and minimal belongings out of the way. Existence is a nightmare; permanence a dream. 'We have forgotten how to dream,' Kalu Das tells me.

Singhajan Ghat lies almost directly across from the tea-trading town of Dibrugarh on the south bank of the Brahmaputra. The floods triggered by the quake of 1950 had devastated the town and its famed tea gardens. A revetment was proposed to shore up the south bank and Dibrugarh, to protect its considerable assets in the tea industry.[2]

In 1954–55, a dyke was built along the south shore using 21,000 cubic metres of stone and 25,000 logs. No such investment was made on the north bank. Fortifying one side and not the other meant that when the river swells, as it does every monsoon, it finds itself hemmed in on the south. The river therefore pushes north where there is no fortification; the bank on that side, along with the agricultural lands, paddy fields and homesteads beyond, are submerged. This process of piecemeal destruction continues with each passing year, the river eroding more and more land to the north, destroying lives and livelihoods.

But come to think of it, it is not the river that destroys, but what we do to the river that triggers the destruction.

Dykes, revetments and embankments as methods of controlling floods are relics of colonial thinking. Assam alone has 4,400 kilometres of dykes, some over sixty years old. A dyke's stipulated lifespan is twenty-five years; those in Assam are now well into their afterlives. Weakened by the constant onslaught of the surging waters, they are only too ready to give way. Moreover, embankments, by design, sever important lateral connectivity between the floodplains, wetlands and the river – connections that are essential to the health of the riparian ecosystem.

When an embankment is built, it is designed to cut off the river from its natural banks. This also means that it is separated from the lakes and bogs that are connected to the river. Floods replenish these lakes, fish from the river seek these wetlands for breeding, the vegetation these areas support acts as a filtration system for the river water, and the silt carried by the flooded river gets deposited on the banks, providing much-needed annual rejuvenation of the food bowls. Some of the choicest paddy grows on these floodplains. Cut the lateral connect of the river with the floodplains and you lose all these benefits. The silt has nowhere to go either; it therefore stays in the main stem of the river, raising the riverbed or increasing silt islands, and eventually exacerbating floods as the level of the river rises.

For all these reasons, experts hold that dykes, ostensibly constructed to contain swollen rivers, cause more damage than they are intended to prevent. Villages huddle in the lee of these dykes, clinging to the false sense of security offered by government assurances that the river will leave the people unharmed. But age and neglect render the dykes increasingly ineffective against the water's wilful strength. Sooner than later, the immense pressures causes the weakened structures to breach. The river races inland, swallowing villages whole.

22 August 2014. 12:30 p.m. The midday meal is being served in the Lower Primary School of Rekha Chapori, a village in

Upper Assam, when the local dyke begins to crack. Built decades earlier, it had weakened with the passage of time, compounded by official neglect.

The Brahmaputra, straitjacketed by dykes and further constricted owing to the Bogibeel bridge downstream, follows the innate nature of water and carves for itself a path of least resistance. Its natural strength augmented by the monsoon, the river contemptuously sweeps aside the ageing, enfeebled dyke and swamps the land, careening through thirteen villages, washing away homes, homesteads, farms, even a hospital.

Rekha Chapori is directly in the path of the river's headlong rush. The headmaster, alerted by the thunderous sound of the collapsing dyke, rushes the children to higher ground. Minutes later, the river rushes through, taking the entire school in its wake. Only a single bench, a funereal memento mori of the cataclysm, is left unscathed.

The river claims twenty-one families of Rekha Chapori, along with their homes and every tangible reminder of their existence. After the cataclysm is over, it is as if the village had never been. The handful of families that manage to survive the flash flood now live with the remains of the day: dead stumps of areca nut trees, a few bamboo mats – a grey existence under plastic tarps of blue and yellow and orange.

'Have you any idea how hot it feels under that plastic?' asks Suseel Kuli, a Mishing. Mishing (Mising) are an indigenous tribe of Assam and Arunachal Pradesh, recognized by the name 'Miri' in the Constitution of India. 'Look around you – do you see how we live?' He waves his arm, spanning a cluster of homes with bamboo mats for walls and roofs of plastic tarpaulin, perched on top of the embankment's ruins.[3] I peek into a hastily pitched house. There is nothing inside except a kettle perched on a brick.

The losses from the flood are estimated at between two and three lakh rupees per family. The government announced compensation to the tune of ₹35,000 – which the victims will receive after two years, maybe more.

Traditional Mishing houses are built on stilts, with roofs of kair grass that keep the blazing summer sun out and cools the insides of their dwellings. These houses now lie under several feet of gunmetal-grey sand. The stilts poke out from the sand at all angles, like a row of misshapen teeth. Sand dumped by the rampaging river has buried the kitchen gardens that were once the mainstay of Mishing self-sufficiency. Nothing will grow in these parts for the foreseeable future.

The survivors live on a knife's edge. The floods contaminated their water sources; they no longer have access to clean water. One rusting hand pump coughs up brown mud and even the occasional fish. Suseel Kuli waves his hand in the direction of Dibrugarh, the nearest big town. He and the other surviving men from the area will have to go to the city to find manual labour for meagre daily wages just so their families can eat.

Seasonal floods apart, there is one additional danger that passes unnoticed – the butterfly effect, with a twist. The mountains fringing the horizon belong to the state of Arunachal Pradesh. The government, in its bid to 'develop' the northeastern parts of the country, has been blasting through these rocks, laying roads to connect the valleys of the river Siang which flows in from China where it is called the Yarlung Tsangpo, the Great River. To power this frenetic construction, the government has permitted –

even encouraged – the mining of rock from the mountains and riverbeds.

When a boulder is removed from a riverbank, the sand that is trapped below it comes loose. The river sweeps the freed sand along; over time this creates cavities into which the river water flows, gradually carving a new path for itself. This divergent pathway widens as each boulder is removed and each ton of sand released. The river, which once carried fertile silt, now rushes towards the plains bearing a new, undesirable load: sand.

In Upper Assam, an area lush with paddy fields, the farmer knows to look to the mountains for the first sign of rain, to identify the flashing signals of a monsoon river in spate. He has learnt from his father, who inherited the same knowledge from his father, that it takes six hours for the rain-fed river to reach the plains. In that time, he makes his preparations, securing his chattel and cattle alike and moving it all to higher ground.

He knows – or rather, knew – the art of surviving, of living as one with the river. But not any longer; now he has no idea how many boulders have been removed and from where; he can no longer tell with the wisdom of generations what path the river will take, or how much time he has.[4] Maybe the river will avoid his land this year; or perhaps a mile away, entire fields and habitations will be demolished. He is no longer sure of the verities of his existence.

So it was in 2015 with the Simen river. It took only one hour of rain in the mountains for the river to flood the plains. One hour's worth of notice, not six. At 1 p.m. on a monsoon afternoon in July, the river, rerouted by changes upstream, wandered a kilometre off its normal course, brushed aside a weak embankment and flooded some of the choicest paddy fields in these parts. It destroyed crops, but something far more devastating took place: it dumped massive quantities of sand on the floodplains, burying an earthmover, smothering the fields and rendering them uncultivable for the next several years.

Such dustbowls are increasingly common in Upper Assam, forcing farmers out of their traditional livelihood and into uncertain daily wage work and deep debt. Standing on a remnant smudge of tarmac which used to be a bustling road, a farmer stares across a stark expanse of grey that was once green with fresh paddy. 'Once this river used to bring us silt. Now it only gives us sand.'

Kapilash the boatmaster is in his sixties, with a fifty-six-inch barrel chest sitting atop bowed legs, his thighs and calves of carved granite. He never walks, but trots everywhere, like a little hyperactive rhino. This son of a Bihari boat-maker was born on a hand-hewn dugout; it is the only home he has ever known. He is at one with his *naao* as well as the river on which it plies, reading its moods and vagaries like none other can. His peers proclaim he is the master of all boatmasters.

His strength is evident from the ease with which he hefts boxes of vaccines, pills, potions and assorted medical paraphernalia and stacks them neatly on the prow of his boat. He then retires to his cabin, high up on the prow. This is home; it holds a bed and blankets, lifejackets and a variegated assortment of fishing nets, net shuttles and twine, a stash of betel nut and another of beedis, and finally his cellphone. It is all a cosy rumple, and it offers a fine view.

The boat, the once deep blue of its paint weathered by time and the elements into the washed-out look that is the dream of denim makers, has its name emblazoned in red on its left side: 'Akha', hope. A crew of doctors, nurses and lab technicians, the carriers of that hope, clamber onboard.

The Boat Clinic is the brainchild of Sanjoy Hazarika, a soft-spoken, thoughtful research professor and journalist. Funded by the National Rural Health Mission, it is ready to set out on its assignment to the remote villages on the chaporis in the eastern reaches of the Brahmaputra. The denizens of these sandbars, with no access to the healthcare facilities of towns and cities, depend on this monthly clinic for diagnosis and medication. The healing boat was unable to make the trip the previous month due to the monsoon; this trip is therefore doubly crucial.

The itinerary is uncertain. If all goes well, we will travel nine hours upstream to the first medical camp, then another four hours to the next before docking for the night. The weather is inclement. Clouds, fecund with rain, loom over us, casting a dull grey smudge over boat and people, river and air. From his perch, Kapilash navigates, reading the river's depths in its countless shades of grey.

He yanks the tiller hard left, the wheel screeching in protest as the heavily greased chain carries the command to the rudder aft. The boat veers slowly into a channel of current, distinguishable by its darker shade. We traverse half a kilometre, and it gradually becomes apparent that the boatmaster had sensed, and steered clear of, a long, crocodile-shaped sandbar that now looms before us.

Darker shades, I deduce, mean deeper water. 'There are no rules,' Kapilash grunts, negating my attempt to reduce his art to a digestible, and therefore repeatable, template. 'It is all experience.'

We are close to the shore, the boat straining upstream against an eddying current. 'This is a game of *saahas*,' Kapilash says. That

Hindi word he uses walks a tightrope between 'courage' and 'daring'.

'You see that – as if the water is boiling?' He points to the middle of the river, where the water bubbles over into ripples that spread across the surface. 'It is shallower there,' he explains. We steer clear of the bubbling water until, with no visual cue I can pick up, Kapilash senses that the sandbars will materialize closer to the shoreline, and veers the boat away towards the middle of the river.

The wind is a steady nip that tugs at clothes and stings the skin, punctuated by occasional humid blasts. There is mist on the horizon; as we watch, it condenses into a dense fog that billows towards us. 'This *kohra!*' Kailash mutters, his forehead creased with worry. 'That's a killer. When there is fog and darkness, you should never be out on this river.'

He calls to his colleague, also a master, and the two discuss the situation in a torrent of animated Bhojpuri. The river is dangerous by itself with its shifting sandbars and variable depths; to navigate it while engulfed in dense fog can be lethal. The boatmasters decide we have to dock.

Kapilash guides the boat towards the shore, but the midstream current is too strong for the engine, and it renders the rudder useless. So the boat is pushed backwards. It has no brakes. To fight one's way upstream is hard enough; to be pushed downstream against one's will, with the added risk of ramming into the massive logs from the dense Assam forests carried along by the currents is hazardous beyond imagining.[5] 'Put one brakeless boat into the path of such a log and …' Kapilash shudders, decides the consequences are beyond his powers of description, and tugs the wheel hard left.

We continue the downstream drift, but the engine gradually gains traction as the current weakens. Kapilash has got up from his seat, throwing his considerable bulk at the wheel as he fights the current. He whips a hand off the wheel to point to an almost imperceptibly lighter patch of grey water.[6] He guides the boat into that patch – a sliver of current that only he could have spotted. The boat catches it, the engine groans in relief as the burden on it decreases, and we start to chug upstream. A colossal log, possibly the result of illegal felling deep in the forest, floats by phantom-like, a grim reminder of the dangers we face. It is 3:30 in the afternoon. Kapilash drops anchor, takes up his fishing nets and goes off to indulge his passion and, hopefully, also to net us a meal.

We have stopped at a chapori. This is a mature, seemingly permanent sandbar with vegetation and a Mishing settlement. It has a name: Phansidiya, or 'gone to the gallows'. The British executed people here, the locals tell me, though I could find no such reference in historical records. The ten-member medical crew set up a tent and unpack the kits. A line of Mishing women, babies slung over their backs messenger-bag style, queue up in front of the tent-flap.

Coughs, colds, fevers and skin ailments of varied types are diagnosed and treated; polio and measles vaccines and tetanus shots are administered; squalling babies are soothed with practised ease; allergy medicines and sundry syrups are handed out; antenatal checks carried out; folic acid tablets supplied to those who ask.[7]

In the summer, the river channels shift and become unnavigable, making it harder for the boat clinics to reach these villages that have no other means of availing medical aid. It is equally difficult for the sick to find a boat that will take them to the nearest health centre.

Going overland is not a viable option either. In the winter of 2017, in a bid to get to a fishing boat that could take me upriver from Jorhat, I had stumbled on foot eight kilometres over a succession of silt islands, along riverbeds and across sandbars, weighted down by my camera equipment. The terrain, as I would discover at the cost of aching calves and thighs, can tax the fittest; it is this terrain that the sick, the elderly and the pregnant have to negotiate if they want to access even the most basic healthcare.

Three hours on, the last of the patients is sent on her way with medicines and advice. A rosy-fingered twilight descends around us as we pile back into the boat for our return journey. Kapilash is back at his post, peering into the darkness, scanning the unpredictable river, reading its myriad dangers, steering his boat deftly past obstacles the rest of us cannot sense. I watch appreciatively a master at his trade. Does he enjoy his work? 'I've grown old doing this,' he grunts. 'What is there to enjoy?'

He throws his weight on the wheel yet again, and the boat swerves left, then right, skipping nimbly past obstacles both underwater and on the surface.

Now the twilight turns to night. The Brahmaputra fades to black.

PART 3
AN ERODING MARGIN

ON THE BRINK OF BRINE

It's no fish ye're buying – it's men's lives.

WALTER SCOTT[1]

WATER SLAPS AGAINST THE SIDES OF THE SEVENTY-FOOT METAL boat, the *Golpata*, as I descend the ladder on its side and step onto a smaller, almond-shaped wooden vessel in total darkness.

It is August 2014, and the monsoon season is upon the delta. There is no moon; the river reflects a cloche of a billion twinkling stars. The chizzzzzz of crickets is an almost meditative backdrop punctuated by the tokey-tokey-tokey call of the tokay gecko and the gentle splosh of oars slicing into water as Mujibur rows away from the *Golpata* and the boat arcs, in a graceful ellipse, into a tiny *khal.*

Mujibur is my guide, spotter, coffee-maker and oarsman. The khal we enter is among the last of the offshoot channels before the many tongues of the Sela river open into the Bay of Bengal, in Bangladesh.

The channel we row through is narrow, and hemmed in by towers of pneumatophores – aerial roots that act like snorkels for mangrove trees – ghostly-white in the glow of my flashlight. Some shoot straight up like spear points, others curve in the air, some are stumpy and thick while still others have curlicued designs on them. Each belongs to a different species of mangrove tree, but their purpose is the same – they help the trees breathe during the twice-daily dunking in brackish water as the high tide pushes the sea in.

Calcified star-shaped cones of barnacles cling to nipa palm trees (after which our boat, the *Golpata*, is named) just above the high tide mark. Huge mud crabs and tiny pink fiddler crabs scuttle and bury themselves in the ashen mudflats that shine in my flashlight's reflected glow.

As we go deeper into the khal, the dense vegetation leeches away even the little light there is; we are in a blackhole where sight is useless and the only sense left is aural. Some sort of creature walks on leaf litter in the forest to my left, its steps going chush-chush-chush. Two bright green circles of tapetum flash briefly and vanish just as quickly. The boat creaks ahead, the reflected stars dance in its wake and the tide continues to rise.

We are deep in the Sundarban, the largest unbroken mangrove forest in the world. They call it the 'land of eighteen tides'. It is the part-forested, part-settled delta of three mighty rivers – the Ganga, Brahmaputra and Meghna – and straddles the border between India and Bangladesh.

Mangroves are both land reclaimers and builders. The rivers of the Indian subcontinent that originate in the Himalayan range are soupy with the silt they accrete and cart across thousands of kilometres, making the Ganga and Brahmaputra among the siltiest rivers in the world.[2] They offload some of the silt along their course, creating fertile floodplains and food bowls before they end up here in the Sundarban. This is where the silt settles, layer upon layer, enriching the soil and creating a conducive environment for the mangroves.

The mangrove's roots – some hanging low like talons, some spreading far like tentacles, others upturned like gnarled fingers poking out of the water – grab the silt and fashion islands that over time link up, eventually merging with the mainland. These islands of silt are technically neither land nor water; they are suspended in the middle realm, ready to be reclaimed at will by the river and rushed into the sea. These ephemeral marginlands balance precariously between the sweet of the river and the brine of the sea, and form the coastal defence against the cyclone-prone 'beating heart of monsoon Asia', the Bay of Bengal.

The Bay is known for the viciousness of the storms it unleashes each monsoon – Sidr (2007), Aila (2009) and Amphan (2020) are merely the best-known examples. These cyclones bring with them sea surges – giant walls of water fifteen feet high – that race inland and sweep aside people and houses, boats and farms and everything else it finds in its path. It is the mangrove swamps of the Sundarban that can abate such surges and lessen their impact on the hamlets inland. The snaking roots of the mangrove cling to the mudflats, anchoring them in place and keeping the soil from being washed away.[3] The turgid sea batters these mudflats and dissipates much of its venom into the impassable barrier of the dense mangroves, which bear the lash of wind and the surge of tide that would otherwise strike at the cities of Khulna in Bangladesh and Kolkata in India which sit along the Sundarban's northern boundaries.

This soupy, silty, eternally shifting landscape is a burgeoning nursery of life where, among the mangrove roots, fish grow, prawns spawn and crustaceans thrive. These mudflat forests have sustained humans for centuries, providing fertile waters for fishing, forests of timber, and flowers for wild honey.

Ruling over this idyllic environment is the storied hilsa, an Indian shad that swims upriver to spawn and lives out its adult life in estuaries like the Sundarban. It is a monsoon fish and a cultural icon of Bengal. No wedding feast is complete without it. The hilsa is the centrepiece of Durga Pujo, the autumn festival that celebrates the goddess Durga in the region. As a travel writer once said, 'If Bengali cuisine were Wimbledon, the Hilsa would always play on Centre Court.'

Everywhere I have gone, I have met Bengalis who would tell me of bygone times when they could plunge their hand into the Meghna or the Podda rivers (the Ganga takes the name Padma in Bangladesh, which in Bengali is pronounced pod-da) and come up with a shimmering 2.5-kilogram *ilish maachh*. An elderly lady in Kolkata once told me that they don't take the fish's name when they step out to buy ilish. 'I'm going to get him,' they instead say, and the message is never not clear. But increasingly such narratives are tinged with a forlorn nostalgia as this king among fish disappears from its habitat.

Back on the *Golpata* which is moored in the middle of this khal on the cusp of the Bay of Bengal, we sit down to a dinner of curried prawns and vegetables, fried eggplant, pappadams and lentils. A sudden gust turns the boat into a rocking chair. The *Golpata* is clearly not meant to be a sea-going vessel. 'Our boat will not last two days in these waves,' Alom, the boatmaster, says.

About a furlong ahead, we spot a large, traditional wooden fishing trawler (not one of the mechanized ones that are the bane of all artisanal fishermen) bobbing in the waves. Butterscotch-coloured buoys are piled up on its deck and, in the weak light of swaying yellow lanterns that throw more shadows than light, we see several men silhouetted against diaphanous white fishing nets.

After dinner, we pull up alongside. The silhouettes grow faces which fill out in smiles of welcome. More men come out from the cabin amidships; we are now close enough to read the name of the boat – *Mayer Doa* ('mother's blessings').

The trawler's cook opens a door aft of the boat, carved with a *kolohi* or *kalash*, and fires up his stove to make laal saa – the red, milk-less tea that is a mandatory accessory for conversation.

A man in his mid-thirties comes forward and introduces himself. Sultan is the boat's owner, a hilsa fisherman operating the *Mayer Doa* with his crew of fourteen. The most lucrative fishing window is in the monsoon months when the freshet in the rivers is strong and the hilsa swim against it, going upriver to spawn. In days gone by, the season was so lucrative that fishermen specialized in the hilsa; in season, they made so much money that they did not have to work for the rest of the year.

Sultan's boat is in its first season. He had bought it for thirteen lakh taka (about $15,000); the specialized hilsa nets cost a further ten lakh taka (roughly $12,000). Sultan is deep in debt, but it wouldn't have mattered if the season was conducive. It has been anything but – the *Mayer Doa* has been on the high seas for two days now, and they have just ten kilograms of hilsa to show for their labours, not even one fish per crew member. Sultan's debt now looms ominously, a crushing burden he knows he cannot overcome.

'When we were young,' says Noor Miyan, an older crew member, 'we'd go out for an hour and come back with enough fish for a day. But now we go for eight hours, we fish deeper, farther out, and still come back with less than half the fish compared to my younger days.'

Between sips of laal saa, Alom offers up a story from earlier that day. We'd met artisanal river hilsa fishermen (Sultan's crew hunts hilsa in the high seas rather than the riverine part of the estuary), three to a boat, who had stretched their nets across the width of the Sela river and waited over six hours. They managed to net just one solitary hilsa. Sultan and his crew nod – they too have experienced it; their peers say that the river is empty this year.

Commercial trawlers and overfishing are two of the culprits. About fifty kilometres off the southernmost tip of the Sunderban is a large swatch where the seabed falls off steeply into a long, narrow canyon rich in marine life – the Swatch of No Ground, it is called. Large trawlers drop their nets deep into this canyon and scoop up everything, indiscriminately – including tiny fish and other sea creatures of no use to anyone. The trawlers toss the bycatch back into the sea and return with ever-decreasing hauls as the indiscriminate fishing depletes the fish stock.

On the way back from the Sundarban to Dhaka, we stopped at Khulna. I clambered down into the icy hold of another artisanal sea-going hilsa trawler. The glassy, baleful eyes of two silver-and-pink hilsa stared back at me from a vast bed of ice – that was all the crew had to show for their labours. For artisanal fishers, up and down the delta that year, the hilsa was nowhere to be seen.

It is the national fish of Bangladesh. '*Podda nodir ilish*' or 'hilsa from the Padma river' makes any Bengali worth their salt salivate. Connoisseurs claim that they can tell the difference between hilsa caught in the sea and that from the Padma. In India too, restaurants regularly import Podda nodir ilish – and not just in West Bengal. The Bangalore branch of Bhojohori Manna, a restaurant chain specializing in Bengali cuisine, imports fifty kilograms of ilish every ten days during the season.

Hilsa is also an 'auspicious' fish, hence its centrality to weddings and religious festivals. In seasons such as this, when the catch is sparse, Bangladesh typically protects its market and bans export. Restaurateurs in India, anticipating losses running into lakhs of rupees, raise their prices. The hilsa-loving Bengali will pay handsomely for even 100 grams of Podda nodir ilish.

The hilsa, a flashy, curvy fish decked in silver scales, is good-looking. It is bony and hard to eat; it is said that a true Bengali can take a mouthful of hilsa and spit out only the bones, stripped clean of flesh. This is South Asia's own salmon: beautiful, beloved, prized, anadromous – and threatened. There is one key difference: unlike the salmon, which is easily farmed in abundance, the hilsa has thus far not taken to being reared in fish farms. It is essentially a wild fish that refuses to be tamed.

Daulatkhan, a town in the district by the same name on the Meghna river, is one of the main hilsa landing sites in Bangladesh. 'We would have had no time to talk if you had come last year,' an auctioneer told me. But on that September day in 2014, the market was almost empty of both fish and customers. Two rows of massive wooden crates were stacked upside down. In a good year, they'd be brimming with shivering fresh-caught hilsa; fishermen would be carrying new loads from the river and upending them into these crates; the shouts of the auctioneers and the clamour of customers would have contributed to the controlled cacophony. In a good year in Daulatkhan, lakhs of takas would change hands in a day. This, however, was the worst hilsa season the delta had seen in over three decades.

The Indian sibling of the Podda nodir hilsa, while acknowledged as less tasty and therefore not as prized, used to make up for the shortfall in the Bangladeshi variety. Hilsa from the Bay of Bengal were known to swim fast against the wild, muddy, gushing monsoon freshet, up the Ganga, all the way to the Yamuna in Agra and even Delhi. Buxar, near Allahabad, was once famous for its hilsa catch. Fish catches in Allahabad used to be between 1,500–2,000 kilograms per kilometre in the fifties and sixties.

The Farakka barrage, a dam 2.2 kilometres long, was built in 1971 in the town of Farakka, where the river bends south towards the delta. Among other things, the dam halted upriver migration of anadromous fish like the hilsa. After the seventies, hilsa catch along the Allahabad stretch of the river vanished, going from twenty tonnes to nothing. A lucrative industry was wiped out along the stretch of the Ganga spanning Uttar Pradesh and Bihar. Upstream of the dam, whole fishing villages found themselves shorn of their livelihood.

Dasharathji, now pushing seventy, is a veteran fisherman and respected village elder in Kahalgaon in Bihar, about 100 kilometres upriver. 'We've been here about 200 years,' he says. 'This is our hometown.' His family traditionally ferried cargo and people in big boats. They also fished, and the catch was plentiful. If they put out their nets at 8 a.m., by noon they would catch 100 kilograms of fish. Packed in ice from Bhagalpur, it would be transported as far downstream as Nabadwip and Chinsurah in West Bengal.[4]

'One year, there was so much … so much hilsa!' His face breaks into a toothy smile at the memory. 'It sold for just one rupee a kilo, and still no one to buy!' These days, hilsa caught in Indian waters rarely weighs a full kilo, and sells for around ₹800, with the price for choice cuts rising as high as ₹1,500–2,000 during the festive season. The river's stock of fish, Dasharathji says, has depleted in both biodiversity and abundance.

Several studies bear out his lived experience. Fish stocks have plunged to 70–90 per cent in the years after the Farakka dam came up, and hilsa has disappeared altogether. It can now be found only south of the dam. Traditional fishers swear that the hilsa caught south of the Farakka comes nowhere close in size and quality to the fish found before 1971, or even to the

A griffon vulture meets its end on collision with the blades of a windmill in the Thar Desert. Instances of the critically endangered great Indian bustard similarly dying have also been recorded.

Mining in the Thar Desert is converting a rich ecosystem into a dust bowl and a true wasteland.

In spite of receiving just forty cloudy days in a year, the pastoralists in the Thar Desert have forty names for clouds.

'We are landlords to bed and beggars to rise,' say the people living upstream and downstream of the Farakka Barrage, who often lose everything to the changed behaviours of the interrupted river.

An endangered Indus dolphin comes up for air in the Beas Conservation Area.

The last of the harpoon fishers in the Brahmaputra collaborate with dolphins to fish. As fish populations diminish and river fishing becomes increasingly unviable, this practice, too, nears its end.

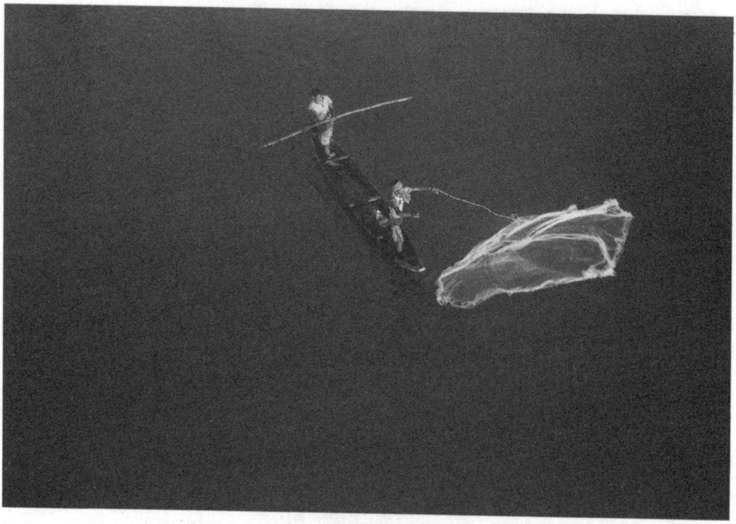

Fishers cast a net in the shallow waters of the Brahmaputra in Upper Assam.

Wetlands are vital fishing grounds for the people living in the Ganga–Brahmaputra basin. Here women fish with the *tongi-jaal*, a dip net.

Twice daily, the tides recede to reveal anemones and zoanthids, which shine like jewels in tidepools off Baga beach, in Goa, India.

Bombay's western coastline is hemmed by rich reefs and rocky tidepools. Reclamation efforts and the new coastal road threaten these important but fragile ecosystems.

When a cargo ship rammed an anchored oil tanker in the Bangladeshi Sundarban, twin disasters ensued: a fragile eco-sensitive area was covered in heavy fuel oil and it fell upon local fishers and their children, like the twelve-year-old girl shown here, to clean up the toxic sludge.

Each year over fifty people fall prey to the Bengal tiger in the Sundarban, leaving behind women dubbed 'tiger widows'. Vilified as bad omens and bereft of any means of income, they struggle to make ends meet.

All along Valiyathura's eroding coastline, homes have been lost to the sea, leaving thousands without shelter.

The endangered black-necked crane, sacred to Buddhists.

The prize-winning ice stupa built in 2019 by the villagers of Shara, Ladakh

Fishers all along the west coast of India are finding their beaches threatened by erosion.

The Brahmaputra starts off as Yarlung Tsangpo, flowing as a thin cerulean film eastwards through the Tibet Autonomous Region, in China, before bending south to enter India as the Siang.

The Lotus Valley in the Hidden Land of Pemakö

The Yang Sang Chu, known as the secret river, flows through the holiest lands in all Buddhism, the Hidden Land of Pemakö, Arunachal Pradesh.

variety harvested in Bangladesh. Moreover, the fall in catch has driven fishers to desperation; juvenile hilsa, called jatkas, are now being netted in vast numbers. This in turn further depletes the population of the adult hilsa.

Dams and weirs, concrete barrages, canals and diversions, pollution, increased sedimentation due to deforestation in catchments, destruction of wetlands that are breeding grounds for fish, and overfishing are the biggest threats to migratory and non-migratory fish populations and biodiversity across South Asia. The hilsa has disappeared from the Cauvery, hilsa fisheries have all but collapsed in the Narmada; and their numbers have dwindled to dangerous lows in the Godavari delta. In Pakistan, hilsa finds its spawning ground on the Indus severely threatened by multiple barrages.

Indigenous fish populations in South Asian river systems have collapsed. Scientists find it hard to put a number on how many species may be lost, as there is little baseline data. Many species not even known to science may have already been lost. The social fallout is that millions of fishermen all across South Asia have plunged into debt.

As Alom and I discuss the various pulls and pressures on the land and its people, he guides the *Golpata* into a cove shaded by nipa palm. There, half hidden from view, we find two little thatched dinghies; two fishermen are huddled inside one of them. Rain falls in white veils around us as we pull up alongside. 'The pirates came last night,' one of them tells us. 'They began to beat up my brother. We begged them to let him go. They did, but they took our trawler. Now we have five days to come up with 5,000 taka as ransom.'

We meet a boy a few days later, the son of a hilsa fisherman. A few months prior, he had been kidnapped and held for nine days. 'I was on a boat; to where would I escape? The only thing to do was wait.' The kidnappers fed him once in two days. On the appointed day, he was finally released after his parents showed up with 20,000 taka.

The pirates are said to maraud in strength, thirty to a boat, three speedboats operating together. They are armed with Chinese-made 0.22 rifles; they hide in khals by day and speed around at night, looking for vulnerable fishermen. They take kids, men, trawlers; their prisoners are held on the chars, to be returned for a ransom: 20,000 taka to a lakh for a human; 5,000–10,000 taka for a trawler. The only silver lining is that if you fall into their hands once, it is as if you win a get-out-of-jail-free card – an assurance that the pirates won't bother you again.

Rumour has it that the gangs operate with impunity accorded to them by powerful politicians, that bloody fights break out between rival gangs, that the coast guard and police are in on the racket. There is reason to believe that some highly ranked policemen even run these rackets to earn back the bribe they would've had to pay to get posted in the city of their choice. Some of these gangs are from India, according to the fishers; others speak of a woman who leads the most feared of the gangs. They don't attack tourists because the resulting publicity can turn up the heat; artisanal fishers, on the other hand, are easy prey.

We pull out of the cove and re-enter the Sela river just as the veil of rain lifts. The river here is a few hundred metres wide, reducing the mangrove forests to a thin green stripe on the fringes. The river is calm, its tea-coloured surface reflecting the thick cumulonimbuses above us. 'Shushuk!' Alom points to the left, a broad grin on his face. A pair of Irrawaddy dolphins crest the river.

Suddenly the *Golpata* abandons the centre of the river and veers sharp left. A ship the size of a three-storey building bears down on us. Some distance behind it, making a right on the horizon, looms another. Then one more. They keep on coming: massive oil tankers and noisy cargo ships, churning through the Sundarban. 'The usual waterways have silted up,' says Alom, referring to Ghasiakhali, a river channel once used for shipping traffic and now so overrun with shrimp farms and embankments that the silt, with no place to go, clogs the waterway.[5]

In December 2014, three months after my first trip, I returned to the region to document a tragedy foretold. I am back on the *Golpata* again. It is 5 a.m.; a dense, impenetrable fog hangs sullen around us. Visibility beyond the prow drops to near zero, forcing us to dock mid-river.

Around this time, on the similarly fog-bound day of 9 December, the oil tanker (OT) *Southern Star–7* was docked four kilometres from the confluence of the Sela and Passur rivers, near Mrigamari, with its hold full of furnace oil. A cargo ship, also plying the same channel, rammed into the *OT Southern Star-7,* which spilled 358,000 litres of black, viscous furnace oil into the river.

The village of Jaymani, at the mouth of the Sela, was the hardest hit as the oil washed ashore. Boats stranded on the mudflats were coated black from prow to stern. Knee-deep in reeds, a woman and a child scraped up the dark goo into a bulging aluminium kitchen pot. Young kids, some just nine years old, funnelled it into corrugated sheets that shimmered over hastily built fires. The heat would release the oil from the vegetation and be collected into a drum to be returned to the state-owned oil company from where it came. Blue-grey smoke rose acrid and potent from the fires; a toxic fog hung low over the fishing village. And the high tide, when it arrived, swept the oil into rainbow-coloured spills over khals 80 kilometres downstream.

OT Southern Star-7 was hardly the first or the only ship to capsize in the Sundarban. Eight vessels, carrying all manner of cargo from cement to oil to potash fertilizers, fly ash and coal, overturned between March 2013 and April 2018. Since then, there have been several more mishaps on both sides of the India-Bangladesh border. In the first seven months of 2020, eight ships carrying fly ash have capsized in the Hooghly which runs along the Sundarban on the west. Three coal ships capsized in 2021 in Bangladesh, and three more have emptied their bowels into the waters around the Sundarban in just the first three months of 2022.

Ruinous as this is, the worst is yet to come. India and Bangladesh have jointly decided to build not one but two coal-fired thermal power plants about fourteen kilometres north of the Sundarban, within sniffing distance of a dolphin sanctuary. Increased shipping traffic carrying coal and fly ash along the river system will soon be the order of the day.

Late at night, we steered towards the centre of the Sela river, close to where the oil tanker had been disemboweled.

From our resting place in the middle of the water, I could barely make out the trees and khals closer to shore. I lay on the boat deck with the stars above and the metronomic lap of the rising tide below. It was an idyll, the moonless night hiding the many dire issues afflicting the region; it was easy to forget the harsh realities undermining the survival of Sundarban's denizens.

The call of the tokay gecko in the distant forest harmonized with the soft voices of Mujibur and Alom as they dined. Dinner included a fresh catch of shrimp acquired from a passing fisherman.

Walter Scott's words played in a loop in my mind.

JEWELS BY THE SEA

A RHYTHMIC BASS BOOM PULSES THE AFTERNOON AIR FROM ACROSS a narrow stream. A beach, swarming with people, stretches in a bright corn-coloured swathe away from the left bank. Two of the several score shacks lining the beach have opened early, signalling their availability through loudspeakers that squawk at full volume. Revellers – mostly men – mill around, beer bottles in hand, awaiting their turn on jet skis and parasails. Smoke from grills laden with assorted meats spirals up to form air sculptures. Offshore, fishermen haul in their midday catch from the Arabian Sea, straining to drag their dinghies ashore against the ebbing tide. Blindingly white cattle egrets, crows and black kites hang above the boats, looking for scraps.

A road signpost that reads 'Sunset Point' hugs the right bank of the stream. I climb up through a straggly scrub outcrop and descend on the other side, onto the basalt and lateritic rocks that hem the shoreline.

Here the sea roars and the gulls call; the vroom of jet skis occasionally rips the air. An angler is perched on the tallest of the rocks jutting out into the sea; his long line is rocked by waves. A couple snuggles in the shade of a rock overhang. Two truant schoolgirls in grey-and-white uniforms giggle and share secrets under the sun. A sullen boy of about seven drags a stick over the rocks, slashing at the pools of water as he walks past.

I step over the jagged rocks, steering clear of the mossy green parts. One carelessly placed foot, I have learnt from experience, can send you flying only to land hard on your bottom. I pick my way past the debris – beer bottles, cigarette butts and shards of broken glass – of the night's revelries and head towards the rocks at the water's edge. Around me, a tide laps the shore gently on its retreat.

'I'm doing a recce for a shore walk tomorrow – want to join me?' Abhishek Jamalabad – whom everyone calls by his last name – is a marine biologist based in Goa. It is early February 2020, and the moon is almost full. For the next few days, the spring tides will rise higher and ebb lower. The low tide will pull the sea out farther than at any other time of the month, leaving behind ocean life in the rocky depressions. The almanac shows the tide will be at its lowest by mid-afternoon.

We meet at Baga Beach at 3:30 p.m. Jamalabad is a slight man in his late twenties. Dressed in a faded T-shirt, cargo shorts and Teva sandals, he carries his camera in a backpack; I get the impression that, as a graduate student, he would possibly have been top of his class. He leads the way to a tidepool and squats beside it.

Blending in with the sandy bottom of this pool, a blenny – a little fish about the length of my pinkie – darts into a rocky crevice and comes back out again. A territorial surgeonfish, looking sharp in its navy blue and lemon yellow, patrols the tidepool until the next high tide sweeps it back into the sea.

'Zoanthus.' Jamalabad points at what look like green pincushions. The little circular creatures shine in hues of emeralds and purples. As the tide recedes and they are exposed to air, these zoanthids shut tight; as a fresh wave douses them with brine they unfurl, waving their tentacles and feeding. Inside each little Zoanthus lives algae, symbiotically, which imparts a colour to these marine animals. In front of us, in a tiny patch of the tidepool, they glow orange, neon green and a deeper leaf green morphs. Elsewhere we come across purple ones. 'I've seen several colours while diving,' says Jamalabad, but the reason they come in so many colour-forms to colonize rocks cheek by jowl is uncertain.

'Don't touch that,' yells Jamalabad as I reach out with one hand to steady myself against a rock. 'Palythoa,' he says, this time pointing at what looks like drab, dusty-brown pincushions. 'They are toxic.' He tells me there is a Hawaiian legend about a shark god associated with it, but he can't really recall it.

Google fills the gap. Like all legends, this one has many forms. The most common version goes like this: Late one evening, as the outrigger canoes returned to the harbour at Hana, in Hawaii, an anguished wail rent the twilight. Another fisherman had gone missing.

This latest incident confirmed the local suspicion that a hunchback hermit who lived on top of the cliff overlooking the sea was to blame. So the fishers clambered up the cliff to confront the hermit. They manhandled him, yanked his cloak off his shoulders, only to and recoil in surprise and fear. On the hermit's back they saw a gaping mouth with a row of triangular teeth.

Their worst fears had been proven true – this, then, was the shark god. They recalled how every day, after the canoes had set out, the hunchback would stroll past the villages and go for a swim. And every day when the canoes returned, there would be one fisherman less.

The enraged fishers set upon the hunchback and tore him to pieces. They burnt his flesh and threw the ashes into a nearby pool. In time, small brown anemone began to appear on the walls of the pool – little creatures so toxic that even a light brush of the spear-like tip of their tentacles could kill. They acquired a name: 'Limu-make-o-Hana' – the seaweed of death from Hana.

These are not in fact seaweed, but colonies of coral called *Palythoa toxica*. The toxin, common to almost all species of Palythoa, is a fatty alcohol that is lethal even in small quantities. Jamalabad has saved me from severe poisoning, or worse.

'Come,' Jamalabad calls, moving to another tidepool. 'There's an eel.' I inch across, careful to avoid contact with the Limu. The tidepool he has found is large, pockmarked with multiple coves.

Poking out from under a flat rock is the black-and-white reticulated head of a juvenile honeycomb moray eel, curious yet cautious, unsure whether to stay or hide. I manage to snap one image before it opts for caution and goes into hiding.

These eels are not studied extensively, but anecdotal evidence shows that they love shallow reefs and near-shore areas. It may have spawned somewhere close by and found itself in the tidepool when the tide ebbed.

By now, we are as far out on the rocks as this lowest of low spring tides will allow. The basaltic rocks directly to the south look like they have been carved into compartments, row upon neat row of chambers with rock walls. In some places the rock walls of the tiny chambers seem thin enough to break off by hand. The layout looks too regular for it to have been caused by wind or tidal erosion alone.

'Urchins,' Jamalabad calls out, following the direction of my gaze.

This young marine biologist is a man of few words, so I do some quick research to learn how those soft-bodied spiny balls – sea urchins – can chew through rock. Sea urchins have five teeth, each arranged in a separate jaw and capable of self-sharpening and regenerating throughout their life. These globular creatures colonize rocky reefs en masse and are often seen snugly embedded into stony pits. So perfectly do they fit in that researchers have wondered if these creatures chew through the rock themselves.

An American researcher, Michael Russell, studying purple sea urchins, found something astonishing: sea urchins burrow into the rock as they chip it away with their constantly sharp teeth. So determined and efficient are these spiny balls in their quest for food that they eat their way straight through rock.

Russell's investigations revealed that on average, across rock types, sea urchins can generate over a hundred tons of sediment per hectare per year. Cumulatively, across all purple sea urchins, this sediment generated by their erosion equals the load carried by many North American rivers.

We climb higher, seeing signs of life on every rock face – semi-circular scrapes of a snail, oval-shaped outlines of limpets, masses of barnacles and some faint marks left by tube worms. At one point we come upon a canyon, its walls buffeted by the now-rising tide. About ten feet above the water is a band of white: hundreds of barnacles, their cones adhering to the sheer rock, surviving where no other sign of life can be seen.

That white band marks the surf zone – a height that is safest from predators, yet washed by the tidal currents that brings them food. The barnacles would have chosen that spot when they were still larvae, yet to develop the adhesive needed to hold fast and the carapace to protect them from crashing waves. They would need to find a place low enough so the tide could feed them, yet safe enough that they would not be washed away by the surf's force. Through my binoculars, I notice that the exposed colony of barnacles have shut their shells tight to the salty air and are waiting for the tide to turn.

I settle down beside an oblong tidepool. A light-footed crab scuttles away from me and disappears into a crevice. As my eyes adjust to the pool walls, I notice another crab, and then one more. A red egg crab languidly waves a pincer at me.

Two perfectly symmetrical cones, furrowed off-white and green, sit at the edge of the pool. Two others lie inundated. Their shape reminds me of the hats worn by Manipuri farmers. Limpets. They hold on to rocks with a fleshy suction cup. This allows them to be rooted, but not sessile.

It was the original polymath Aristotle who, sometime in the fourth century BC, pointed out that limpets are not stationary creatures, that they go forth to forage. When the tide comes in, they let go their suction and allow themselves to be carried away. After feeding, they return with the tides to their original spot. How some species of limpets are able to home in so accurately, finding that exact oval residue left by their suction on one rock out of thousands, remains a mystery. I watch the two limpets in front of me. The tide is rising. Perhaps they are readying to let go.

On a far rock, a thunder-grey reef heron rocks its neck back and forth as it high-steps around tidepools, looking for a meal. In the distance, a bright late-evening sky silhouettes a boat anchored in the sea. Hunting terns lift off and dive into the water. On a spit of sand, gulls sit facing a stiff wind.

All around me are rocks that will soon be submerged by the spring tide, the highest the tide will rise this month. The name of the tide has nothing to do with the season but is derived from the Saxon word 'sprungen' – to spring forth higher.[1]

The shore I am on is ancient, possibly over ten million years old, formed in the mid to late Miocene. The earth was humid then, leading to intense weathering of the ancient basaltic rocks, forming iron-rich soil and revealing the lateritic lowland plains of India's coast between Mumbai and Thiruvananthapuram.

This margin of land and sea – a constantly shifting, eroding, accreting shore – is far older than these pocked rocks, dating back to when the Indian plate, then a part of Gondwana, broke off from East Africa and drifted eastward to collide with the Eurasian plate. Sustaining toxic corals and sprightly eels, barnacles and urchins, crabs and herons, this ancient shoreline is very much alive. To perch on these rocks is to feel the rhythms of the earth itself.

As I watch the tide roll in and swallow tidepool after tidepool, reclaiming its treasures, I think of what we are doing unto the wild coastline of India.

When those of us from the city think 'wildlife', we only imagine megafauna: elephants, tigers, wolves, leopards, lions, whales, dolphins, sharks. This may be due to any number of factors: what's commonly shown and spoken of in the media, the charisma of these creatures, the rise of the photography-craze, popular fables, blockbuster films, and even ancient mythology. People planning cities too probably fall prey to such thinking, disregarding the treasures at their feet, in the depressions of rocks on the seashore. The true intertidal zone – the area that is submerged and revealed twice daily by the neap tide – is often missed in the sweep of the eye from beach to waves to horizon.

About four hundred kilometres up the west coast of India from where I stand, sprawls the sixth most populous metropolitan region in the world. Mumbai, with its press of twenty-three million people, has a long coastline, much of it rocky and similarly studded twice daily with jewels in tidepools – each treasure trove different from the previous, each a fresh surprise, in spite of the sewage and waste water, oil spill residues and trash that wash up on its coasts every day.

Citizen groups, in a bid to introduce Mumbaikars to their own backyard wilderness, conduct shorewalks according to the lunar cycles (when the low tide is lowest).[2] Octopuses, moray eels, stunning multicoloured nudibrachs, myriad anemone, worms, bivalves, sponges of unimaginable colours among countless other sea life appear regularly at the feet of curious citizens. It would be a wonder if anyone who goes tide-pooling would come away less than astonished.

But the narrative of economics and business trumps the treasures of the shallow seas and deep oceans in the commercial capital of India. The powers that be have decided that Mumbai would do well with another eight-lane highway, smeared over the coastline.

At the time of writing, nineteen of the proposed twenty-nine kilometres of hyphenated tarmac, purported to ease traffic congestion between the north and south parts of the megalopolis, has begun to smudge out the intertidal zone. Mumbai stands to lose out on not only rich marine biodiversity but is also putting in jeopardy its first human occupants – the traditional artisanal fishing community, the Kolis.

Over a hundred hectares of land will be filled up and reclaimed from the Arabian Sea. In a vertical city, where between two-thirds and three-fourths of the daily commute is by public transport, one wonders why a road that will cater to the transport needs of a smaller, more privileged section of society makes socio-ecological sense over shoring up and improving the widely used bus routes and suburban train lines.

There is also a further clear and present danger facing Mumbai. Of the 136 coastal cities in the world, Mumbai, along with New Orleans, are second only to Guangzhou in terms risk from extreme weather events and rising sea levels. It is estimated that Mumbai could lose hundreds of billions of dollars in damages due to sea-level rise if mitigating measures are not taken in time.

The intertidal zones in Mumbai comprise not just rocky tidepools but also mangroves, both vital to the protection of the coastline as well as to livelihood and biodiversity. Destruction of these marginlands have hurt the megacity in numerous ways in the recent past.

Over the last two decades, violently heavy rains falling in a single day have devastated Mumbai. On 26 July 2005, for example, the city received thirty-eight inches of rain in under twelve hours. The reclaimed low-lying areas flooded over, killing nearly a 1,000 people. Such severe rains and subsequent floods have followed every few years. In the decade following, Mumbai has lost property and infrastructure to the tune of $2 billion and 3,000 people have lost their lives to floods.

The city saw its longest and wettest monsoon ever, as the heaviest rains ever recorded in July lashed with overwhelming force. And then August proceeded to break all previous records for rainfall in that month. On 5 August, eight inches of rain collected in the city in just four hours, double of what is classified as 'violent' rainfall by India's meteorological department. When October came, instead of retreating from India as it is supposed to, the southwest monsoon dropped twice the amount of rain the month had ever seen. Each time, the inundated city ground to a halt.

The reason Mumbai floods is both natural and human-induced. This northern part of India's west coast is susceptible to heavy rainfall. But here's the rub: Much of the city, built on vast tracts of land reclaimed from the Arabian sea that bounds it on the west, lies below the high-tide level. An extensive antiquated network of drains, built 100 years ago by the British, budgeted for just one inch of rain per hour is therefore hopelessly inadequate for tackling the copious rains of recent years.

Besides, only three out of 105 outfalls, or ways out to the sea, are equipped with floodgates. This means that when heavy – even violent – rains coincide with high tides, the sea enters the drains and blocks any outflow through the remaining 102 outfalls. The city goes under for hours and the result is loss of life, property, livelihoods and revenue.

Add to this storm water drains and sewerage systems choked with plastic refuse, encroachment into and destruction of the city's nature-given storm-surge buffers, the mangroves; unplanned development that blocks natural outflow paths, built-over wetlands, and continued reclamation that is flat, low and prone to flooding and stagnation of water.

Adaptation to impending extreme weather events has been slow-coming. For a city that fights devastating flooding every monsoon due to insufficient drainage, a coastal road being built in an intertidal zone should be cause for deep concern. But construction continues unabated, drowning out cautionary voices.

The sun has now gone down and the tide is rising all around me. The zoanthids, closed tight when exposed to the air, are now in full bloom – purple, pink, three shades of green, a brilliant blue – and waving distortedly through the surf.

With a deep sigh I rise and retrace my steps up the hill. The music grows louder; the shacks are now fully open for business; the beach is obscured by what seems like a hundred thousand people; blinding neon lights assault the gentle twilight. As I emerge on the other side of the hill, a full moon rises behind the din.

I pause.

The moon and the tides; the tides and the shore; the shore and the creatures; the creatures and the sea; the sea and humans … We are connected by one elaborate conversation, whether we choose to hear it or not.

EATING UP THE COAST

THE SEA IS A FEATURELESS, UNIFORM ASHEN GREY FROM SHORE to horizon. The sky is a spectacular jay-blue, with wisps of white cirrus pulling at soft fluffs of cumulus. The air is thick, moist, inert – in the absence of the wind, the clouds stay where they are. Across the landscape, there is a sense of expectancy. Everyone waits for the wind to turn, to blow from the southwest, driving pregnant clouds towards land.

As the afternoon wears on, the sea progressively darkens into a deep emerald. Bulbous gunmetal-grey clouds sag over waves that reach ever higher, some climbing as high as nine feet. The wind revs up; the stifling heat of the last few days has been replaced by a perceptible nip that sends a sudden shiver up the spine.

There is something momentous about this scene, a sense that the stage has been set, the props are in place, and high drama is about to begin.

I am not standing so much as swaying on the beach at Adimalathura in Kerala's Thiruvananthapuram district, buffeted by the raw power of the wind. The sea has turned from emerald to a mossy green now, incessant waves crashing against the beach, dissolving each time into a sulphuric ochre froth. The horizon, out to the southwest, has deepened to charcoal.

As if on cue, the rain cascades down in the distance – a thick unbroken indigo veil that drops from the skies into the roiling sea below.

It is the Wall, and this is the first sighting of the southwest monsoon over the boisterous Arabian Sea.

The beach is bare of life. The fishermen, who had earlier in the morning reeled in the last catch of the season, have secured their boats and nets and gone home. The young ones have ended their football games. I am alone here now, my camera set on a tripod whose legs I've driven deep into the sand. The whole assemblage is covered in a plastic wrap.

The wind is unsparing; it whips up the sand and flings it at me; thousands of tiny pellets strike like arrows and settle on clothes and skin and face and hair. The air fumes and rages, sending empty jerry cans and assorted litter flying about the beach. Crows flap their wings frantically but get nowhere. Colours morph, the light drops and shines then drops again, the now-white waves spring ever higher, their tops whipped by the wind into misty wisps.

The indigo veil of rain is still out there over the sea, racing towards landfall. It is yet to hit the shore, but I am already soaked in the spray. The light is now gone. The darkness is complete.

Onto this stage set by the elements enters the Wall. It rushes in from the indigo veil, assaulting me with sprays of tiny-tipped arrows. It is unrelenting, this assault, a barrage of sea spray and sand and furious, ceaseless rain.

The Wall has made landfall on the southernmost tip of Kerala's coast in all its unapologetic, heart-stopping beauty.

The southwest monsoon's landfall is a 'tourist attraction'. People come from all over to watch from the comfort of their rooms in resorts overlooking the beach. Media houses send camera crews to record the spectacle. Breathless accounts feature in books. But when the rains arrive, twenty kilometres up the coast, it is not the monsoon's beauty that the fishing village of Valiyathura notes.

'There was a loud sound in the middle of the night,' says Bindu. 'We rushed out and saw the house to our right falling into the sea.' On a sun-soaked day in October 2019, Bindu, a diminutive woman in her forties, wearing a pink nightgown despite the late hour of the day, takes Prem Panicker and me on a tour of rubble that once was a kitchen, a hall, a bedroom, as a staircase to nowhere rises from the ruins. 'The well of freshwater is gone too,' she tells us, pointing in the general direction of the sea.

As the monsoon intensified that year, Bindu's house began to crumble. The surging waves sliced away the foundations, leaving a hole where the floor of the living room used to be. The yawning space is now packed with sandbags, creating an uneven surface. On a plank bed balanced on these sandbags in the salmon-walled room her aged, ailing father-in-law lies almost comatose, staring blankly at the ceiling. The door, ripped off its hinges, leans against the far wall. Through the half-open window sounds of the angry sea drift in; waves billow high and then break, frothing on the thin spit of beach that remains. Every so often, a particularly energetic wave sweeps through the temporary sandbag barrier, washing over the room and swirling around the legs of the bed. As it retreats, the sandbag floor shifts, and sinks just a little.

'It happened in minutes,' Bindu recalls. They picked up a few belongings and cowered in the far corner of the house, putting as great a distance as they could between themselves and the sea. But the waters kept coming. Ultimately they abandoned the house and moved inland with the belongings they could carry, knowing that there would be no chance to retrieve anything else later.

Officials ushered them to a government school that had been converted into a temporary shelter. There they found eight or nine families from the area, all displaced and sheltering in a single room inside the school building. Bindu's neighbour, who had lost his house, was already there.

'There were all kinds of people,' Bindu remembers with a shudder. 'All kinds … some not so well-behaved.' Drunks. Fearing for her safety, a neighbouring family sent their young girl to their relatives' home further inland.

Local landlords and their touts realized that there would be a demand for rooms. They doubled the advance down payments and tripled rents. Bindu's family could hardly afford it. The monsoon meant there was no fishing, therefore no income either. So Bindu and her folks stuck it out in that single schoolroom, along with others similarly disadvantaged, for three nightmarish months.

The government provided a daily dole of rice and lentils. Bindu requested a relative, whose house was a few lanes behind theirs and higher inland, for the use of their kitchen so that she could cook a meal and carry it back to the shelter. Evenings and nights were fraught, when the men grew more and more inebriated. Finally Bindu's family decided to use up their meagre savings to rent a one-room flat.

The government dumped sand on the narrow spit of land separating their house from the sea and gave each family ₹1000 to sandbag the shore. Better than paying out money they couldn't afford for rent, Bindu thought, and decided to take the chance.

Packing sand in bags and stacking them up as a defensive wall is arduous work; area youngsters refused to do the hard yards for such scanty sums. Paying out of pocket, Bindu's family managed to build a small wall to block the waves, and moved back to their own home. They hired labourers to pump out water from under their floor, stuffed sandbags into the cracks, and crossed their fingers in hope. But the roof tiles were gone, the wall was cracked, and there were no funds left for repairs. When it rained, they huddled in different corners, awake and alert for warnings of another collapse.

'When the winds come, it worries us,' Bindu tells us. 'It was never like this earlier – there were five rows of houses between ours and the sea. But each year, the sea comes in further. All the houses in front of us have been destroyed; now there is nothing to block the wind and the waves.

'We dare not sleep at night. Whenever the winds pick up, I run out to check the skies.'

This deadly game of tag with the sea is playing out in the southwestern tip of the Indian peninsula, the southernmost part of Kerala. The district, which includes the state capital, Thiruvananthapuram, runs eighty kilometres along the Arabian Sea, and stretches inland into the forested Western Ghats. The southernmost tip of the district is fifty kilometres from the Indian peninsula's southern tip, Kanyakumari, abutting a district with the same name.

This is one of the most dynamic coasts in the world and among the most densely populated, with over 2,300 people per square kilometre. During the monsoon season, which begins in late May, this region sees impossibly rough seas – locals call it the '*kalla kadal*' – rogue waves.

The resilience of a coast and the health of its beaches are heavily dependent on the sediments brought by the rivers that empty themselves into it. Forty-one rivers, all originating in the Western Ghats, empty into the Arabian Sea and, over time, all of them have seen their flows diminish for various reasons. Dams interrupt water flow and impound sediment; sand mining drastically reduces silt content; waters are diverted through canals into agricultural areas; deforestation and debris of various sorts choke the flows too.

The consequences of blocking rivers remain unrecognized. The Kerala floods of 2018 are a case in point. Heavy rains on 15 and 16 August that year caused the Periyar river to rise, and the bridge connecting Malayattoor, a village on the northern bank in Ernakulam district with Kodanad on the opposite bank, became impassable. When the waters receded, the bridge – a vital artery connecting the two areas – was found choked with plastic refuse to the point where movement of relief vehicles became impossible. An earth mover was brought to clean up the refuse and clear the bridge. The operators had a problem: a mountain of garbage and no place to dispose of it. They took the easy way out, dumping the tons of waste back into the river.

In the aftermath, there was a political pie-fight with various sides blaming each other, but the real issue – the long-term consequences of such systematic choking of rivers and the consequent reduction of the silt that is carried to the sea – was unaddressed.[1]

The result is that the only sediment transportation – which builds and maintains beaches – takes place by wave currents. The 'longshore drift' is a current that transports sediments up the west coast of India, flowing south to north off Kerala during the non-monsoon months. These are gentler, milder currents compared to the monsoon drift, which reverses direction and flows south.

A misguided policy, based on outdated science that did not take into consideration the hydrology of the coast, saw Kerala build seawalls and groynes over half of its 590-kilometre-long coastline. Over time, these interventions exacerbated the very problem they were supposed to solve: coastal erosion.

Where a seawall on India's southwestern coast juts out to the sea, it obstructs the sediment-carrying currents. The northern drift of sediments, which is vital, for it deposits its load of sand that shores up a beach, is halted by these concrete or stone structures. Sand accretes to the south of the structure; consequently, no sand reaches the north. This deprives beaches to the north of much-needed replenishment ahead of the monsoon season. When the monsoon comes, there is less beach to stop the surge of the sea; the tides therefore increase in power and sweep whatever is left back into the sea. And thus, progressively, the coastline erodes with every passing year – and with each such spell of erosion, the sea creeps nearer to the homes, as in the case of Bindu, who has seen five entire rows of houses destroyed by the sea before it attacked her own.

It is for this reason that Kerala has seen severe erosion – a whopping 63 per cent – of its coastline. Experts argue that there is no scientific evidence that the coast would have eroded without seawalls. Instead, the linear hard structures have ended up causing erosion where there was none before, and have transferred the problem up the coast and all the way to Karnataka. Whereas worldwide there has been a gradual rethink of these hard structures on coastlines, Kerala continues to build seawalls, dooming what's left of its beaches.

On Adimalathura beach, a group of fishermen are engaged in shore seine fishing – *kambavala* or *karamadi* in local parlance.

A boat takes a massive net out to the sea and drops it in a wide arc. The net is attached to a braided jute rope over three inches in diameter, the ends of which are held by fishermen on shore. The currents bring the fish; as the net fills, the fishermen on shore begin to haul the net in.

It is a labour-intensive process. Two rows of fishermen, one at each end of the rope, bend low to the ground, pulling the ropes to the rhythmic chant of '*hai-ho-hai-ho*'. It is a vigorous game of tug-of-war between the fishermen and the sea. The tide pulls the bulging net backwards at every ebb; for each yard the fishermen gain, the sea pulls the net back by half a yard. Over forty fishermen are deployed across the two ends of the rope; they range in age from wizened elders of sixty-plus to tykes barely in their teens.

It is a good day; the net is so full that the fishermen struggle against its weight. As I watch, three young fishermen with the narrow hips and broad shoulders of star swimmers strip off their shirts and shorts. Clad only in their underwear, they step to the water's edge. They bend and scoop up sea water in their cupped hands. Then they raise their cupped hands in prayer to the sea, take a small sip of the water, pour the rest back into the sea as libation, before plunging into the waves. Swimming ahead of the net, they push it towards the shore, on the alert to prevent the bulging net from going down under a tide and allowing the fish to escape.

On shore, a group of fisherwomen wait patiently beside large aluminium tubs. The fishermen redouble their efforts, but the net, now nearing the shelf of beach, refuses to budge. Finally, four young men wade in with bright red net bags, which they fill with fish and tow back to shore.

The fish are deposited at the feet of one of the auctioneers on the beach. The women surround the auctioneer; the bidding is intense – being first to market with fresh catch ensures the best prices. As each batch is auctioned, the winner piles her prize into her aluminium tub and races away up the beach, yelling for an auto-rickshaw.

The fishermen, meanwhile, redouble their efforts. The net, which the four young men have partially emptied, is now easier to manage; the chants grow louder as they drag it up the shelf and bring it closer to shore.

Adimalathura beach lies to the south of a large breakwater that thrusts into the sea to protect the Vizhinjam port, one of Indian industrialist Gautam Adani's many maritime projects. Because it is to the south of the obstruction, this beach has been accreting sand and growing, thereby facilitating shore seine.

As you head north, the story changes. Shore seine fishing – kambavala – has very nearly vanished along this part of the Kerala coast. This type of fishing is important, especially for ageing fishers who can no longer spend days out on the seas. Sardines and mackerel, staples of the Kerala diet, are the chief catch.

But shore seine fishing requires sizeable stretches of beach – and to the north of Vizhinjam, the beaches are eroding at an accelerating rate owing to the breakwater's effect in blocking the flow of silt. The raging tides of the monsoon season carry sand out to the sea, as is its nature; the silt-carrying currents of the non-monsoon season do not reach the northern side and replenish it. Thus the beaches deplete by a few more yards every year. There are now fewer beaches to the north where kambavala fishing is possible.

For fisherfolk, the beach is home. This is where they park their boats and stretch their nets out to dry. There are no guards, no security – the fishers respect each other's property, and the honour system prevails. Each fishing village has its stretch of beach; it is where they land their catch, where the women buy the fish at auction and race for the markets.

This is a delicately balanced ecosystem.[2] The auctioneer maintains a running tally; at the end of the day, when all the catch is sold, he totals up the day's take. His commission comes out first; another sum is set aside to meet the costs of mending nets and fuel for the boats. The remaining amount is divided among the forty or so fishermen involved.

When the catch is meagre, as it often is, there is very little money to go around – sometimes a fisherman will end up with just twenty rupees to show for hours of backbreaking labour. It is the women who supplement this scanty income by selling the fish in the retail marketplaces of the nearest towns and cities. Break any link in this chain, and the whole system collapses.

Now that there are fewer beaches with sufficient space for kambavala operations, the men can't fish, the women have no catch to sell, and entire families and fishing communities are pushed to the brink. Having no beaches to start from, fishing communities are now forced to truck their boats to beaches in

Guruvayoor or Vizhinjam, risking direct conflict with the local communities.

The very breakwater that is allowing sand to accrete on Adimalathura beach obstructs any littoral drift northward. The breakwater thrusts some 600 metres into the sea as of this writing, with a plan to have it reach three kilometres.

There are other knock-on effects of a linear structure of this kind. Almost all the stone for the Adani port at Vizhinjam will be quarried out of the ecologically fragile Western Ghats. The Adani Group has obtained licences to 2.5 hectares of a quarry site near the village of Nagaroor – the Kadavila quarry – from where it is slated to drill and blast out more than 2,30,000 tonnes of stone over five years. Kerala has been plagued by landslips, suffering 115 large-scale landslides between 1983 and 2015. Seventy-eight of them were within a kilometre's radius of a functioning quarry. Since 2015, 60 per cent of major landslides in the country has occurred in Kerala alone.

From source to sea, development seems to be hellbent on flouting the rules of nature and undermining the resilience of the land.

Two doors up from Bindu's house in Valiyathura, the sisters Sheba and Sunitha squat outside the mangled ruins of what was once their home.[3] Their daughters and an aged father potter about inside. Their husbands are out at sea.

It used to be a two-bedroom house; since the 2019 monsoon, a living room and a kitchen are all that remain. Exposed brick and protruding iron rods mark the place where their bedrooms used to be. Those rooms have collapsed into a mass of rubble; doors have fallen off and lie askew on the ruins.

'We were born in this house,' Sheba says, on a blazing hot morning in October 2019. 'We were married here; we gave birth to our children here. This is the only home we have ever known.'

When they were younger, Sheba recalls, their home was well away from the sea. There was an expansive stretch of beach, and three rows of houses ahead of theirs. Over time, the sea encroached. It eroded the beach and, during each volatile monsoon season, marched further inland, destroying each successive row of houses. Now their ruined home is in the first row, separated from the sea by a few feet of sand.

Those whose houses had been destroyed earlier live in limbo. In 2012, after one such wave of destruction, the Congress-led government launched a scheme to build thirty-two homes for the fishing families who had been affected. As of October 2020, only eight homes have been built; the remaining families have been sheltering, for eight long years, in a refugee camp. And their numbers grow with each passing year, as successive monsoons destroy more homes and leave more families shelterless.[4]

Earlier, the sisters recall, the waves would rage every monsoon and carve their way inland, but the beach would rebuild itself every summer. 'Now the sand never comes back,' Sheba tells us. 'Our beach is gone.'

They invite us indoors to see the damage for myself. Wooden rafters on the roof have been torn away, exposing half the living room to the sky. A bright yellow wall, all that remains of one bedroom, faces the sea in a last act of stubborn defiance.

The sisters ask us to drink tea with them. 'We don't have milk – will you take it black?' We refuse, pleading that we have just finished breakfast. The sisters are chatty; they discuss the weather, the depredations of the sea, the fragile nature of their existence, all in matter-of-fact fashion, smiles constant on their faces.

You must visit us again, they insist as we take their leave. I promise. 'Who knows if the house will still be standing, whether we will still be here? But take our number,' Sheba says. 'Call us when you come back.'

We make our way out, making a mental note to return during the 2020 monsoon – but the pandemic plays havoc with our plans. A call will have to do.

'The yellow wall you'd seen,' Sheba says, 'that went first. The waves kept coming; the rain poured in through the roof. The living room began to vanish, little by little. It's all gone now – only the kitchen's left.'

Theirs is a joint family of seven people, including one ailing elder. They want to move away and rent a place. 'But where can we go?' Sheba says.

Valiyathura, a suburb of Thiruvananthapuram, is a small fishing port. Houses that have rooms on rent are few and far between; most have been occupied by those who lost their homes in the last two years. Touts, sniffing an opportunity, have raised the rents of the few houses that remain to near-unaffordable levels.

During the peak monsoon period, the area was a Covid-19 hotspot. 'No officials came to check on us during the monsoon because of Covid,' Shebha says. And no help is forthcoming.

The thin spit of beach in front of their home is gone. The sea comes right up to their kitchen now. They squeeze into that tiny space, and they wait.

'Come visit us soon,' are Sheba's last words before the line goes silent.

THE TIGER'S LAIR

GULALBIBI HAD TWIN CHILDREN – A BOY, SHAH JONGOLI, AND A girl, Bonbibi. For the poor family, a girlchild was an unwanted burden, so Gulalbibi abandoned her in the forest. Soon a herd of deer came across the child; from then on, the deer became her family, and Bonbibi grew up as one of them.

Elsewhere, the forest-dwelling Brahmin Dokkhin Rai, known as 'the king of the south', grew increasingly besotted with his power. Possessive of his fiefdom, he refused to share its resources with humans and began, in the guise of a tiger, to prey on anyone who wandered into the forest. Following his example, the tigers of the Sundarban began predating on humans.

When Allah noticed the plight of the humans, he summoned Bonbibi to his presence. Around this time Gulalbibi, stricken with remorse, went with Shah Jongoli into the forest in search of the daughter she had abandoned. On seeing her brother, Bonbibi told him that Allah had a mission for them. Taking leave of a tearful Gulalbibi, the two children trekked to Mecca in obedience to the divine summons.

When they arrived at the tomb of Fatimah, daughter of the Prophet Muhammad and his first wife and follower Khadijah, to seek her blessings, a voice issued from within: 'During times of trouble, 18,000 souls will call out to you for help. They will call you mother. You will respond with kindness, and rescue them.'

Taking an oath to do as she was bid, Bonbibi returned to the Sundarban with her brother, and a titanic struggle began, first against Dokkhin Rai's mother Narayani and then against the 'king of the south' himself.

As Bonbibi gained the upper hand, Dokkhin Rai sued for peace. Bonbibi assured the locals that in return for their devotion to her, Dokkhin Rai would leave them unharmed. Humans, for their part, would have to enter the forest 'empty-handed' and 'pure of mind and intent'.

From this legend springs the locals' unalienable belief that the settled part of the Sundarban, comprising fifty-two villages, is under the protection of Bonbibi while the other fifty densely forested, uninhabited islands are the realm of Dokkhin Rai. There are shrines in every village dedicated to Bonbibi and Shah Jongoli; they also mark the roads and paths to the river.

The belief cuts across religious divisions; Hindus and Muslims alike are devoted to Bonbibi, the forest goddess revered as the protector of honey-collectors, woodcutters, fishers, crab-catchers and anyone else who benefits from the forest commons. Before setting out into the forest, every fisher family prays to Bonbibi.

'I've stopped worshipping Bonbibi,' says Sunanda, a slender five-foot-six, as she expertly mends her nets.

She recalls how, on the morning of 22 November 2011, she woke up feeling weighted down by an anxiety she could not put a finger on. Her nine-year-old son Bappaditta's middle-school exams were two days away. Her second son Bibekditta had just started going to school. As she busied herself getting the kids ready, her husband Nabin announced that he was heading out into the mangrove forest to fish.

The Forest Department mandates that fishermen have to go three to a licensed boat, armed with fishing permits. Since his brother-in-law Gopal had other plans that day, Nabin rounded up two other companions and set off around 10 a.m. Sunanda remained at home, in the grip of her inexplicable unease.

Early in the afternoon, the headmaster called Bappa out of his classroom and told him to go home. The youngster, a promising student who was particularly proficient in Bengali, protested. Exams were imminent, and he wanted to study. 'Go home,' the headmaster insisted. 'We'll handle the exams later.' Perplexed, Bappa went home to a surprised Sunanda.

They noticed a commotion in the village. The word 'accident' carried to them over the jumble of agitated voices. The head of the panchayat called on Sunanda. He informed her that the boat had come back.

A fishing trip usually lasts seven to ten days. Sunanda was alarmed, and the vague anxieties of the morning intensified, enveloping her in a blanket of dread.

She learned of the incident in bits and pieces. Nabin's long, narrow boat had entered a khal and attempted a three-point turn to negotiate a particularly sharp bend. A tiger, sensing opportunity as the boat came close to the shore on the turn, had pounced, snatching Nabin off his vessel and carrying him into the forest. His two companions gave chase but failed even to recover the body.

Life as Sunanda, Bappa and Bibek knew it was over.

Giving her nets a final once-over, Sunanda straightens and calls out to Bibek, a four-foot-nothing, reed-thin boy in a frayed blue sweater and brown shorts a few sizes too large for him. He emerges from the bamboo-and-mud hut carrying a large yellow bucket. Sunanda rolls up the nets and an assortment of sticks and poles, and perches the bundle on his head. Bibek walks ahead towards the clay embankment.

'Take your sandals off,' she tells me, frowning at my feet. 'You will lose them in the swamp.' Carrying the yellow bucket and some shallow metal trays that look like they had come from the surgical ward of a hospital, she follows after Bibek. I kick off my sandals and trudge along behind them.

It is a full moon day in February 2017, that time of the month when the tide ebbs further, exposing more of the mudflats, before surging back higher. For Sunanda, this is a monthly window for hunting mud crabs and harvesting prawn fingerlings.

Sunanda and Bibek climb the embankment and walk into the swamp on the other side. I follow. Within the first couple of minutes, the word 'walk' – to move forward, as the dictionary defines it, at a regular pace by lifting and setting down each foot in turn, never having both feet off the ground at once – appears to be a misnomer. It would be more apt to say that I wallow, flounder, lurch, stumble … My thesaurus, which I check later, confirms it.

In the swamp, underfoot conditions are uncertain. Put a leg down and it sinks halfway up to the calves; lift the other and, in that moment, when all the weight is on one foot, it sinks deeper. I fight for balance and hastily put the front foot down, and it immediately sinks almost up to the knee. All of this is to the accompaniment of embarrassing sound effects – the slurp-burp-wuchuck as you pull your foot out of the muck, the liquid plop as you plant it down, the squelch of my trail pants covered in goo, the involuntary yelp of pain as a foot lands on a stone or the sharp stump of a withered tree.

Sunanda and Bibek walk ahead as if they are on the smooth pavements of my residential enclave in Bangalore. We move deeper into the heart of the world's largest unbroken strand of mangroves. It is dark and damp, with only the occasional shard of sunlight slicing through the thick overhead canopy. The ebbing tide exposes pneumatophores, the snorkel-like roots that help the trees breathe during the twice-daily dunking in brine at high tide. A blue mist hangs about the trees; jade-green spirals of snails cling to the barks just above the high-tide line. Mosquitoes the size of marbles swarm overhead, whining and whirling around like little motors gone berserk in some sci-fi flick.

We wade through the rivulets that snake among the mudflats, pushing deeper still into the forest. I struggle to keep pace with mother and son, then give up the attempt and make what progress I can. The mud gets softer as the river comes into sight, and 'walking' progressively harder. Unseen pointy objects and the occasional sharp-edged rock make covering ground an exercise in pain management. Bubbling patches of mud signal the presence of quagmires – to be avoided at all costs.

The edge of the Datta river is finally visible: a soupy sliver of khal about four feet deep, flanked by ashen mudflats leading into the dank mangrove forests. Veins of such silty khals meander across the Sundarban; seen from above by a drone, it resembles nothing so much as a deep green nest of snakes.

Straddling the border between Bangladesh and India, the forests of the Sundarban carpet the Ganga–Brahmaputra–Meghna delta, where the three rivers branch out and re-branch and branch out again into a thousand tongues before emptying into the Bay of Bengal.

Built by silt carried from the Himalaya by the Ganga and the Brahmaputra rivers and from the east by the Meghna river, this is a vast delta. Much of West Bengal and Bangladesh are formed of this delta, prompting the geographer Willem van Schendel to say, 'In a sense, Bangladesh is the Himalayas, flattened out.'

The twice-daily ebb and surge of tides alternately inundate the area with brine and expose it to the fierce tropical sun. On the margins of sweet river water and the brackish Bay, across West Bengal and Bangladesh, over seven million fishers, crab-catchers, honey-collectors and farmers engage in a daily struggle for survival.

Sunanda lives on one of the inhabited islands in the southernmost part of the Sundarban archipelago, beyond which lie wildlands teeming with Bengal tigers; saltwater crocodiles; venomous, constricting snakes; endangered birds; primates, crustaceans, monitor lizards, river sharks, river dolphins, anadromous fish, wild boars and deer, all superbly adapted to a life on the brink of brine.

Sunanda and young Bibek wade into the Datta river – the water waist-high for mother and chest-high for son. They jab long poles deep into the riverbed and stretch their nets across; the mesh is so fine that it will trap even the tiniest prawn seedlings being carried by the current.

The threat of crocodiles and the occasional river shark is a constant. Women collecting prawn have had their thighs chewed off; some have lost legs. And yet Sunanda and her ilk, for whom livelihood options are limited, make repeated trips deep into the swamp, throwing in their lot with destiny.

These trips are equal parts hope and desperation – the last resort of the helpless.

Sunanda is just one among many locals to have suffered multiple tiger-related tragedies. She was about ten when she lost her father to the tiger. A few years later, her father's brother was taken. And finally Nabin, whose death left Sunanda with two young sons and no source of income.

She filed an insurance claim, but since Nabin's body was never found, the mandatory seven-year waiting period to declare a missing person dead kicked in. The government-mandated compensation had been held up on the ground that Nabin and his boatmen were allegedly fishing in forbidden waters. The Sundarban is a tiger reserve and large swathes of the forest – its rivers included – are notified as 'core areas', out of bounds for fishers and crab-catchers.

Fishers complain that the Forest Department makes it impossible for them to earn a livelihood by withholding boat licences and permits and unilaterally expanding the 'core areas'. The waters in the buffer zones are devoid of fish or crab, forcing them to go deeper into the designated areas. If a tiger attacks within these spaces, there is no hope of compensation. Worse, fishers who return with news of an 'accident' – the local euphemism for a tiger attack – complain of official persecution. Deaths therefore go unreported; the bodies that are recovered get hastily cremated before a post-mortem can be carried out, and 'accidents' are covered up. The extreme risks are known and yet, driven by hunger and the need to provide for families, fishers continue to take them.

Fifteen years ago, Asit Mandal was out crab-hunting with his older brother and nephew near the mouth of the Bay of Bengal in the wintry fog of December. They had jabbed a baited longline in the mud of a khal when the tide was still high and had gone fishing while waiting for the crabs to bite. When the tide ebbed, they returned to check their lines. Their boat was almost on the mudflats exposed by the ebb.

They had checked about 200 of the 800–900 baited lines. But none of them noticed the tiger on the shore. Asit became numb with fear when the tiger attacked, its paws pushing him into the water. He estimates that he spent eight or nine minutes 'in the tiger's embrace'.

With a vice-like grip on his head, the tiger began to pull him ashore. Asit's panicked brother and nephew grabbed an oar and struck the tiger on its head. The tiger dropped Asit and ran away. The boat by then had drifted into the river and had to be hauled back so that Asit, who had fainted, could be taken home. He remained unconscious for six months; it took several surgeries across several years before he could function again. When he did recover and return home, his face had a zipper-like line of stitches running up to the back of his head and across half his scalp – a daily reminder of that horrific day, a violent scar that would come to define his life.

Today, still traumatized by the incident, he farms his garden, refusing to reclaim his traditional livelihood. 'I cannot ever go into the forest again; it terrifies me,' he says. 'I get goosebumps even when I see it in a dream.'

Official figures indicate that each year over fifty fishers are taken by tigers – an average of one a week. Since many of the attacks are hidden from the authorities, these figures reveal only so much. Left behind are hundreds of women dubbed 'tiger widows', considered bad omens and ostracized into separate enclaves. Support for these women is hard to come by, as no one in the community is ready to offer help. They suffer in their isolation, their trauma unshakeable.

That evening, as I walk back from Asit's home to my room on the far side of the island, a few men stop me. 'We have noticed you walk alone every morning to the river's edge and back again in the evening. Are you not afraid?' I am perplexed. What should I be afraid of? 'The tiger. It hides in the *dhan*,' they say, pointing to the ripening paddy fields. I had not internalized this, despite hearing such stories. As I continue walking, I glance at the fields, noticing a soft wind blowing through the paddy stalks. I feel my steps quicken; my hands clutch my camera tightly, knuckles whitening. My palms suddenly begin to feel clammy as the sun dips behind a wind-breaking row of trees. In that moment I begin to know the fear these people live with – a quiet, persistent gnawing every day and every night.

A pole leans over, bent by the current. Bibek tugs it back upright and secures it, then walks out of the water, shivering in the misty February air. Sunanda trudges back to the mudflats, picks up the hospital pans and wades into the river again, painstakingly scooping up water to harvest the squirming transparent, inch-long, prawn seed.

Away from the river's edge, Sunanda threads a baited string through four four-foot-long sticks, plants them in the mudflats, and waits for crabs to bite. The tide is beginning to come in. Spring tides rise higher than during the rest of the month. Sunanda sloshes through the rising waters, checking her traps. Almost imperceptibly, she tugs the baited string with her left hand, her right holding the blue net-scoop at the ready. No crab. She tosses the bait back into the water and checks trap number two. No crab. Trap three. One crab. Trap four. Empty. By now, she and Bibek have spent six hours in the swamp, defying treacherous underfoot conditions and predators alike – all for a solitary crab.

She tries again the next day, with the same result: a single crab. The tide is waist-high and rising when Sunanda pulls up her traps and wades along a predetermined path back towards the embankment. 'Follow me closely,' she warns, 'or you will be sucked into a quagmire.' Camera held high above my head, fighting for balance, I follow as closely as I can. Even so, I splash, and stumble into a bog. Sunanda's strong grasp steadies me. She fixes me with a glare. 'I'd told you ...!'

Bappa is fifteen years old, and his tenth-grade exams will begin in less than a fortnight. The venue is a high school in the nearest town, Gosaba, fifteen kilometres away. He will need to take a flatbed three-wheeler half the way, then a ferry, and then another flatbed to reach his destination. The exams span two weeks, so he needs to find a room to shack in, and he will have to pay for his food. Sunanda estimates that it will cost a total of ₹2,000 and works frantically to collect the money.

She has farmed potatoes, she is hunting crabs and collecting prawn seed, threshing paddy for a local farmer who, she hopes, will pay her on time. With ten days to go, Sunanda has collected sixty rupees by selling potatoes, one hundred and ten rupees for crabs (forty of which she had to spent on bait-fish), ten rupees selling some greens she has harvested, and thirty-two for her prawn seed. One hundred and forty-two rupees towards her target of 2,000 – and that does not account for the money she and her sons need for food. There is just one spring-tide day left for crab-hunting.

The full moon nights of January and February mark the two biggest pujas for Bonbibi. A few yards down the road from Sunanda's house, the entire village has gathered at the local shrine.

Women chop mounds of fruit to make the sticky-sweet rice that is handed out as prasad. Little barefoot girls shriek and chase each other in their shiny, frilly frocks. Young boys, hair plastered to their scalps with coconut oil, play with marbles and sticks. The priests and other men from the community gather flowers and sundry puja essentials while chanting verses from the Bonbibi Jahuranama. Ten-year-old Bibek sits with a bunch of other kids, enjoying biscuits and sweet ice.

The men and women of the village come forward, one by one, to prostrate at the feet of the goddess and her sidekicks. They offer flowers and ring the temple bells. The priests light three fires. A woman steps forward to stand in front of the idol. The priests place one pot of fire on her head and balance the other two, one in each her outstretched hands. The music and the chanting rise to a crescendo.

Sunanda stands at the back of the throng, a part of and yet apart from the festivities. She watches silently, her face an inscrutable mask. Abruptly, she turns on her heel and walks slowly back towards her home.

Above her, an alabaster full moon rises over the forest.

The names of the tiger widows have been changed to protect their identities.

PART 4

THE THIRD POLE

WHEN THE GLACIERS DISAPPEAR

JAGGED LIGHTNING RIPS THROUGH THE MASSED BULK OF cumulonimbus, shredding the dark of the night. Rain erupts in a fusillade that pockmarks the mountain slopes, gouging out chunks of earth, tattooing the slanting roofs of homes and streaming down in rivulets that merge into a gushing, gurgling slurry of mud that gorges on everything in its path – trees, boulders, vehicles, furniture, all swept up into a giant battering ram that blasts down the incline and bludgeons the cowering town below.

A man scrambling to escape is flattened mid-stride; a mother bent double to shield her baby from the downpour is lifted off her feet by the flash flood that spares nothing and no one in the way, as bushes, trees, homes, people get caught up in the maelstrom from hell.

Ladakhis shudder at still-raw memories of the night of 5 August 2010, when the trans-Himalayan desert town of Leh, Ladakh's capital city, received one year's worth of precipitation in two unearthly hours. Several hundred people died; over 800 went missing.

This wasn't supposed to happen. India's northernmost plateau, Ladakh is over 3,000 metres above sea level, with the Greater

Himalayan Range curtaining it to the south and west. The lofty peaks create a rain shadow in which Ladakh nestles, enjoying over 300 days of sunshine in a year; the region gets at most four inches of rain annually.

'Ladakhis had no living memories of floods,' the soft-spoken Magsaysay Award-winning engineer and educator Sonam Wangchuk says with a shrug.[1] 'The last documented flood occurred in 1933,' he tells me.

Then came an unprecedented flood in 2006 that devastated the Phyang valley. It was followed by the destructive flood of 2010, then another in 2012, again in 2015, and most recently in 2018. Clearly something had shifted – a region that hadn't seen floods in over seven decades was wrecked five times in the space of a dozen years.

The rhythms of Ladakhi life used to be as immutable as the mountains that enfold it. Snow falls here in November and December. The winter sun thaws the snow into meltwater which swells the high-born streams that flow to the valleys, replenishing the burnt-brown grass to create lush, marshy meadows.

Come spring, the snows are spent. The glaciers take over, melting slowly under the sun and releasing their waters to keep the rivers recharged and the grasslands alive. Wildflowers open up to the sun in luxuriant profusion; black-necked cranes fly in to nest in the marshes. Shepherdesses from the high winter pastures descend to the exuberant valleys with their flocks famed for pashmina wool. Crops of barley, wheat and peas, fed by the glacial melt, yield rich harvests.

But all of this is changing. Winter temperatures have risen by about 1°Celsius over the last four decades, and snowfall has become increasingly unpredictable. Glaciers have disappeared from some ranges, while others are shrinking in size and receding to higher altitudes. The higher a glacier is, the later in the year it will melt. Consequently, there is now a months-long gap between the snowmelt of spring and the glacier melt of summer.

Spring, a vital crop-growing season, is now virtually dry, rendering rural livelihoods increasingly unviable. To make matters worse, lucrative dry-land agriculture has been all but destroyed by the central government flooding the Ladakhi markets with cheap white rice from the fields of Punjab. This double whammy has triggered an exodus of pastoralists and agriculturists to Leh, which is already overburdened with ill-planned tourism and ill-equipped to deal with the influx.

The population of Leh was 5,000 about thirty years ago. Now it is 30,000, and at least half are migrants from rural Ladakh. In Leh, I met farmers turned taxi drivers; in the tourism hotspot of the cerulean lakes of Changthang, erstwhile pashmina shepherds were serving tea in lodges. Harvesting the prized wool of the pashmina goat is no longer a feasible occupation, as grazing meadows dry up due to lack of glacial melt. Long lines of migrants from the countryside form regularly outside ration shops and daily-labour contract depots, desperate for food, for work of some kind.

Ladakh is sparsely populated, with a density of just twelve people per square mile as against the national average of 1,042. It is home to pastoralists and dryland agriculturists. Its carbon footprint is negligible; it plays no role in effecting climate change. Yet the region now bears the brunt of it.

Wangchuk and I drive west from Leh, following the Indus river past herringbone valleys that slope down to its banks. Fed by glaciers, the river flows from Tibet into India, then along the length of Pakistan to empty into the Arabian Sea.

The winter of 2018–2019 has been promising for Ladakh. The northern slopes of the mountains are smothered in white. The road we are driving on is flanked by walls of ploughed snow towering eight feet high. As we make our way between these frosty battlements, Wangchuk recalls his moment of epiphany.

It was the summer of 2013. On one of his trips to the villages around Leh he noticed, under a bridge and sheltered from the sun, a large mound of ice that had not yet melted. He gazed at that little stupa of ice, his mind in overdrive.

The word 'stupa' is derived from Sanskrit; it means 'mound' or 'heap'. In Buddhist tradition, a stupa is usually built of stone or mud to house the relics of monks (or nuns), and is a revered place of meditation and contemplation. In Wangchuk's mind was born the idea of a stupa thick with ice, which would mean life itself for Ladakhis. It boiled down to simple physics. Ice turns to water when exposed to heat; the larger the surface exposed, the faster it will melt. But how could one freeze large quantities of water with the least exposure to the sun?

In the eighties, the pioneering Ladakhi engineer Chewang Norphel had helped build dams on streams high above villages, and harnessed the meltwater from those frozen reservoirs for use during the summer. But the dams had to be situated high up in the mountains; building them was therefore backbreaking work. Villagers, heavily burdened with building materials, had to climb hundreds of metres in bone-chilling winter to prep, construct and maintain the reservoirs. Building such reservoirs lower down, closer to the village, was untenable because the ice would melt too quickly and defeat the purpose.

Wangchuk saw it as an engineering problem. It was necessary to store ice at lower elevations; to prevent it from melting too quickly, the surface area exposed to the sun had to be limited. The sight of that small tower of ice under the bridge triggered an idea. 'Eighth-grade maths tells us that a cone is the simple answer,' Wangchuk tells me.

In the winter of 2013, Wangchuk's team piped water from a mountain stream down into a valley in Leh. At the site selected for the experiment, they forced the water to flow up a vertical pipe with a fine nozzle attached to its end. The water went up the pipe and exited through the nozzle as a fine spray. In nighttime temperatures of -30°Celsius, the spray froze as it left the pipe. Gradually, as more and more water emerged as spray and turned to ice, the edifice took the shape of an upside-down cone, an 'ice stupa', wide at its base and tapering towards the top.

That early prototype reached a height of six feet and locked in 1,50,000 litres of water. During summer, the water melted slowly under the sun, lasting until May. Wangchuk now had proof of concept, and was ready to take his idea on the road.

In 2015, Wangchuk and his team built a bigger stupa near the village of Phyang. It contained 1.5 million litres of meltwater, which the nearby villagers used to create a grove of 5,000 willow and poplar trees. 'We should have been more judicious,' says Wangchuk. The trees they had chosen were thirsty trees, wholly inappropriate for the desert ecosystem of Ladakh. As a result, they ended up sucking the water up all too quickly.

As we drive along, Wangchuk points to clusters of wild rose bushes, junipers and capers. 'These native bushes are ideal,' he says. 'They help retain moisture in the soil even when it rains, which seems to be more common now.'

The recurring floods are a constant preoccupation. Wangchuk plans to use ice stupas to restore native vegetation, which will help bind the soil and thus stem the havoc of floods. 'Why should we take these changes lying down?' he asks. 'Let's replant the valleys and thwart the devastation of floods.'

Wangchuk is determined to find a lasting solution to Ladakh's water issues, thus mitigating the effects of climate change, restoring traditional livelihoods and abating the exodus to urban centres. His ice stupa captured the public imagination; in 2016, he won the prestigious Rolex Award for Enterprise and, in 2018, the Ramon Magsaysay Award. Recognition has made him more ambitious, and inspired him to think of larger, more lasting solutions. His dream is to build an ice glacier – a mountain of ice that will replenish itself in winter.

'Imagine,' he says as we negotiate a particularly ice-slick curve of road, 'a stupa ten metres thick at its base. If it loses only five metres during the summer, and adds another ten metres the next winter, it becomes fifteen metres thick by next spring. Again, it loses five metres in summer, adds another ten the following winter and is now twenty metres thick ...' His face lights up with a beatific smile as he contemplates the vision. 'What we will have is a stupa that grows year on year – a true artificial glacier, a perennial source of water.'

Thanks to his growing reputation as an innovative problem-solver, the Indian government has invited him to devise means to drain a glacial lake in the eastern Himalaya. There are 8,000 to 9,000 such lakes formed by the retreating glaciers; about 300 of them have been declared dangerous, with the possibility that they could breach and cause floods downstream. Wangchuk's team is working on finding a way to drain the lake and refreeze the water to create an ice reservoir.

Wangchuk is focused on finding solutions, but the injustice of the situation is not lost on him. 'It is not enough to come up with technical innovations, adapt and solve problems,' he says. 'The root cause also has to change.' He points out how the people of the mountains have to find ways to solve the issues that city people cause with their carbon-intensive lifestyles. 'I want to use ice stupas as much to sensitize the world about the need for a change in behaviour, as I want to use it to provide water for us,' he says to me, his words considered.

His problem-solving mindset extends beyond water-related issues. In the village of Phey on the banks of the Indus, some sixty kilometres south of Leh, Wangchuk founded and runs an alternative school for kids who have failed tenth standard. 'These children are bright; there is nothing wrong with them,' he says. 'The trouble is with the system and the manner in which these students are taught. Education should not become a ritual. If you spend sixteen years of your life doing something, it should help you solve problems. Science should be understood and applied in simple ways.'

The Students' Educational and Cultural Movement of Ladakh (SECMOL) exemplifies his philosophy. The campus was built using low-cost traditional techniques. It is solar-heated and fossil fuel-free. A massive solar cooker sits outside the kitchen area where three students sit with cups of tea, deep in discussion. In the school, science and maths are taught by engaging students in real-life problem-solving. The students manage and administer the campus – planning meals, milking cows, growing vegetables – democratically. Graduates of SECMOL go from being deemed failures to running successful institutions and businesses of their own.

One team of students runs the ice-stupa programme, training villagers in the art of building ice cones through online videos and hands-on workshops. In 2019, the ice-stupa effort attained scale. Villagers from around Ladakh attended SECMOL workshops and built their own stupas that year; to motivate them, the school launched a competition that would reward the largest stupa.

At Karith, a village that hugs the mountainside close to the border with Pakistan, a stupa built by local students won second place. Mohammed Ali, the school headmaster, couldn't afford the trip to Leh to attend the SECMOL workshop, so he and the other teachers watched YouTube videos and imparted their learnings to the students. 'We want to make the children aware of what is happening in the world, how it is affecting us, and what they can do about it,' Ali tells me as he shows me around the school library which is festooned with charts and posters teaching scientific concepts using locally relatable examples.

Attaining this secondhand wisdom about ice-stupa construction involved much trial and error, discovering which ropes and pipes could hold out against the freezing cold and which would give way. But finally, in 2019, the stupa they built at the base of a mountain ridge a mile behind the village stood tall and proud – a blue, curvy cone some seventy-three feet high. Downstream lay terraced fields covered in winter snow but which, come spring, would transform into fields of barley, wheat, peas, sorghum and potatoes. The stupa is big enough that its meltwater will, in spring and summer, cascade down to four villages, bringing relief during the driest months.

Next we land up in Takmachik village, which sits above the Indus, hugging a high cliff of smooth river-burnished rocks. Here, apricot-farming is the main source of livelihood. Building a stupa was a learning experience for the farmers of this village. They have built one, but at a lower altitude, which means that the ice will melt earlier, in May, whereas apricot trees require the largest quantities of water in July and August. Wangchuk huddles with the farmers, listening to their experiences, planning fixes. The farmers invite us into their homes and ply us with salty tea and organic apricots of two varieties, both sweet with a surprising hint of tart. As more villagers join us, the discussions turn to the mountainous terrain upstream of the village. Wangchuk sows the seeds of a solution to be implemented the following year: a series of stupas at different altitudes for a steady source of water through spring and summer.

In the village of Gya, east of Leh, it is the youth who have engineered a stupa, adding to it a twist. Their stupa houses a cafe. Ice spires of different lengths hang from above, reflecting and refracting the light outside, giving the cafe a hue of glacial blue and aquamarine. A menu card lists the items on offer, and a hut to the stupa's left serves as the kitchen.

A sign that hangs askew on the stupa's wall explains the idea behind the structure. Gya is on the route for tourists and birdwatching enthusiasts, who shuttle between the popular lakes of the Changthang plateau and Leh. The cafe thus makes for an alluring wayside stop. Using 70 per cent of the profits, the youngsters chartered buses and took the village elders on a pilgrimage. 'No one takes the senior citizens anywhere,' says Sonam Chosdup, general secretary of a village youth group. They have made plans to use some of the cafe earnings to create a nursery for medicinal plants endemic to the region; this will serve the dual purpose of reviving the ancient tradition of herbal medicine and generating additional income.

In the far-western region of Ladakh, where the district of Kargil borders Pakistan, the district commissioner tells Wangchuk that he wants to build twelve stupas near different villages to keep the lucrative apricot agriculture alive. Thus begins an involved discussion about ways and means.

A few days later, I sit at the base of the largest stupa built in the winter of 2018–2019. This two-tiered ice structure, atop the village of Shara at 4,500 metres above sea level, soars 110 feet high. A local farmer, trained as a mountaineer in the Indian Army, pulls on his cleats and scales the structure to fix a clogged nozzle. A few villages down, a woman farmer, who feels newly empowered on having found solutions to local problems, stuffs my pockets with roasted barley from her field, and asks me to bring her a pair of sunglasses when I visit next.

With each passing year, the building of stupas gains the force of a grassroots movement. This rekindled spirit of community is, to Wangchuk's delight, mostly driven by the next generation. Restoring a love of their own lands, making village livelihood sustainable, stemming the exodus to the city and staunching the fallouts of climate change will, he believes, catalyze a return to Ladakh's former prosperity.

Five months after my initial visit, in August 2019, I check in with the ice-stupa team at SECMOL and ask them about the stupa at Shara. It is peak summer, but only half of the stupa has melted. The ice will last until winter, they tell me, and then it will grow again, crystallizing over itself and increasing in girth and height. Wangchuk's dream of a self-sustaining artificial glacier seems much closer to reality.

In March 2019, Wangchuk and I had driven away from Kargil, hugging the Pakistan border for several miles until we arrived at a checkpost. As an army jawan scrutinized our papers, Wangchuk turned to me with a wry smile. 'We're caught up in conventional notions of defence, imagining our biggest enemy to be Pakistan or China.'

But in the coming years, he mused, we will need to defend against the assaults of nature. Disappearing glaciers. Flash floods.

Droughts. Food shortage. Outmigration. A multitude of assaults that are often clubbed under that common rubric: climate change. 'We need a defence budget, a plan to help safeguard people, landscapes, ecosystems. There is no point fighting over fences in the face of a tsunami.'

A COUP ON THE ROOF OF THE WORLD

DOGS HOWL. UP THE VALLEY, DOWN THE ROAD, BEHIND THE house, below the ridge. All night long a hundred dogs yowl in an a cappella orchestration from hell.

When the indigo sky turns a pale shade of blue, we step out of the still-slumbering Ladakhi house that had taken us in for the night. A chill wind tags the low-hanging clouds, revealing peaks with an overnight dusting of snow. I am in the company of two young naturalists, Harsha and Payal. We are crisscrossing Ladakh, documenting the high plateau's flora, fauna and pastoral way of life. Tossing our rucksacks in the back, we pile into our geriatric jeep.

An army camp sprawls on the outskirts of the village. There are bunkers everywhere. The road skirts a long, narrow strip of bog, across which lies China. It is the summer of 2018, and we are climbing towards a high pass in the vast grassland plateau of Changthang, in India's northernmost district of Ladakh.

A lone black calf comes careening down the slope to our right. There is no shepherd in sight, which is unusual – livestock is the lifeblood of Ladakhis; they usually do not let their flock wander about unsupervised. We drive around a bend in the road and see a second calf on the ground, its neck turned at an unnatural angle, its legs crumpled beneath its body. A thin trail of fresh blood oozes from two neat puncture wounds that disfigure its dark coat.

Three Tibetan mastiffs stand in a rough semi-circle some thirty yards off, licking their paws and watching us warily. One is black, the other two are tan. Their winter coats are falling away in patches; their maws are stained with blood and reddish wet fur clings to their legs. They turn and lope slowly up the slope, abandoning their kill. It starts to snow, the first flakes falling like a benediction on the still-bleeding carcass.

It is summer in Ladakh, the 'land of high passes'. Shielded from South Asia's monsoon by the Greater Himalayan Range that stretches to its south and curves west, this Trans-Himalayan region is a vast, cold desert.

In the southeast is the Changthang plateau, which stretches into the Tibet Autonomous Region (TAR) and sits at an average altitude of 4,500 metres above sea level. Richly biodiverse, it is home to snow leopards, Tibetan grey wolves, Eurasian lynxes, blue sheep, ibexes and the endangered Tibetan antelopes called chiru; one also finds here the argalis, the largest wild sheep in the world, as also marmots, pikas, voles and several species of eagles, owls and vultures. The sacred, highly endangered black-necked crane flies in from China each summer to breed in the bogs of Changthang. The bar-headed goose nests here in summer and makes a perilous journey over the high Himalaya to winter as far south as Tamil Nadu in southern India.

We cross the pass and descend towards a valley, driving past more army camps. An oblong oval of marshland, surrounded by peaks lightly dusted with snow, lies ahead. Short Chang-pa horses in tans and whites and browns and blacks pick their way across the bog, heads down as they graze. Yaks in their thick, dark matte winter coats, and the cattle-yak hybrids called dzos slosh along, their snouts lowered, foraging on the vegetable matter growing in the marshes. Noisy ruddy shelducks fly about in breeding pairs, asserting territory. In the midst of this crowd of fur and feathers stand two black-necked cranes, each about four feet high, caps of red over an attire of pure white, with a trailing plume of black and a matching neck. This nesting pair has likely flown some 500 kilometres from the Yarlung Tsangpo basin in central Tibet, China.

Their nest hides in mounds of grass in the middle of water no deeper than a couple of feet. The cranes spoon up vegetation from the marshes, collecting enough to make a small island on which to lay their eggs; where that is not possible, they collect mud to make mounds. The female lays one or two eggs at a time, and the pair take turns incubating them.

'This year they have laid two eggs,' says Namgyal, a shepherd likely in his forties, who is from the first village down the road from the bog. We sit around a low, carved wooden table on the carpeted floor of his kitchen, sipping salty butter tea. His shepherdess wife and other villagers saunter in and out, offering snippets of information.

The villagers are the self-appointed local guardians to the cranes. No villager will touch the eggs, as any disturbance can cause the parent birds to abandon the nest. Their vigil is prompted by the proliferation of dogs in the region, and the risk of them chasing the nesting birds and stressing them out. The nests of the black-necked crane are at ground level, leaving the eggs vulnerable. Moreover, once they hatch, the rufous feather-ball chicks are unable to fly for several months. This makes them prime targets for marauding dogs.

Feral dogs were earlier not seen in these parts, the village elder Dorje tells me, until the army camps came to the valley.

With their arrival, traditional sheepdogs learned to gorge on human-generated wet waste, of which there was plenty thrown outside the army compounds. Tibetan mastiffs, trained to protect livestock, began to go rogue. They got lazy, stopped guarding livestock and simply lay about, as food was within easy reach at any time.[1] Eventually they moved away from the villages and vanished into the mountains, from where they made forays to the village in packs to feed and, increasingly, kill livestock. The locals are convinced that up in the mountains the dogs mate with wolves. What results is a bloodthirsty hybrid known as Khipshang in some and Parjo in other parts of Changthang.

Historically, dogs were domesticated from wolves, and both have the same number of chromosomes – seventy-eight. Dogs interbreed with wolves elsewhere in the world, and their offspring is fertile. Studies have shown that when such hybridization takes place, the animal tends to lose its shyness, becomes aggressive, and begins preying on livestock. Hybrids have been known to attack humans as well, as successive generations lose the impulses of domesticity and their sense of belonging.

Marauding Tibetan mastiffs are a prevailing danger to Ladakh's wildlife, for they are present in numbers wherever there are tourist or army camps. Wildlife department surveys have counted over 3,000 mastiffs in Changthang alone – an area where the human population, not counting the army and tourists, is under 10,000 nomadic and semi-nomadic people.

Refreshed by the sight of breeding cranes, disturbed by what the villagers tell us, we drive due east past war memorials and army check posts, along the Indus where it enters India from China, past hills painted in hues of olive and amethyst, red and rust, until we find ourselves in a large bowl of marsh mounds surrounded by mountains in serried ranks like so many chevrons, and dotted with little settlements. This is the village of Hanle; our homestay is barely ten kilometres from the Tibet Autonomous Region in China.

Here night falls with a disorienting abruptness, like a black hood abruptly pulled over your head. Such all-encompassing darkness is a rarity in India; there is magic to it, and mystery. Looking towards the sky, it feels as if I am gazing at eternity itself. Exhausted by the day's drive, we soon pass out to the background score of the distant howl of canids.

After lunch the next day, we drive out to explore the valley, past an upland buzzard's nest incongruously adorned with several prayer flags; fluffy chicks of a Eurasian eagle owl; a family of red foxes – mama, papa and three kits – in their den; flocks of sheep and goat and the occasional horse, until we halt next to a nunnery. Crouching low with our cameras and binoculars, we step into the marsh and begin a careful scan of the northwestern part of the bowl, east to west.

Our binoculars sweep past a coffle of all-male Tibetan wild asses locally known as *kiang*; the short mountain horses that proliferate in the region; two shepherdesses silhouetted against the warm orange dust clouds kicked up by the yaks they are coaxing homewards, and towards a white Chang-pa tent called a *rebo*. A second sweep picks up movement between us and the tent. We focus, and see a shape in the grass, bent over, tearing at a carcass. It lifts its head, and we gaze into the face of a Shangku, the Ladakhi name for a Tibetan grey wolf.

It wears an emaciated look, whether from age or hunger we can't tell. Its winter coat is frayed. As we watch, a black Tibetan mastiff bounds through the marshland into the frame and stops some distance from the wolf. The wolf backs off from the carcass; the mastiff moves forward a couple of steps. Now the wolf steps forward; the mastiff retreats just a little. This dance of dominance continues until a second dog, a white mastiff, appears. While we watch through our binoculars, we are too far to hear the threatening barks.

The two dogs work in tandem, pressing the wolf hard. Eventually the wolf gives up and lopes away. The dogs approach the carcass, but do not touch it. Once the wolf is out of sight, the dogs backtrack to the place from where they had come, somewhere to our east.

A hunting wolf expends a lot of energy. If denied the spoils, that energy is wasted and they are forced to hunt again. Kleptoparasitism, which is parasitism by theft, is a phenomenon whereby one species of animal steals the resources – food, nesting materials – of another. It is a frequent occurrence in the wild, but the coming of dogs as competitors is a new and dangerous threat for the endangered Tibetan wolf. This is especially true in lean times, and more so when the density of dogs is high in the home range of a wolf.

As the sun sinks behind the mountains and we make our way back to the homestay, we meet a group of pre-teens who have been brought to Hanle by their school for an outdoor camp. Tents go up in the meadow adjacent to our homestay; music blares from a set of outsize speakers, and kids mill around, unloading backpacks and foodstuff from two buses.

As if on cue, the dogs turn up. One has a mangy beige coat, another a tan winter coat that is peeling off. A big black mastiff with its tail in a tight furry curl, clearly an alpha, stalks into the centre of the group. They are hungry, and the smell of food from the snackpacks is tantalizing. The campers shoo them away; they shrink back a few steps and flop onto the grass, biding time.

Over dinner, we tell our hosts Sonam and Padma what we have just witnessed. Sonam's expression is grave. A few months ago, he says, a pack of dogs took down a Eurasian lynx. The dogs also got the chicks of two pairs of black-necked cranes that had nested in the nearby bogs. Another pack of dogs attacked a lady in a village close to where we were staying; she died of her injuries. It was not the only instance of dogs attacking humans, I learn.

A guide attached to the wildlife department at Leh had warned us of such incidents before we set off. A departmental survey across Changthang in early 2018 recorded one army camp where dogs outnumbered army personnel three to one. The survey showed that free-ranging dogs were killing more livestock than snow leopards and Tibetan wolves combined.

Local herders have begun to feel the pinch. Dogs used to prey on smaller livestock, notably sheep, but have now begun targeting larger animals like calves and dzos. Loss of livestock is covered under an insurance scheme offered by conservation programmes, but only if the depredation is effected by a wild carnivore. Dogs, however feral, do not count as wild animals, and therefore herders don't get compensated for the livestock they lose to these predators.

The steadily mounting loss of livestock is changing local attitudes towards wildlife. Earlier, when a snow leopard took a goat or a sheep, herders accepted the loss and availed of the compensation. But the increasing pressure on their herds has hardened their outlook; they are less inclined to be philosophical about the occasional predator, and this has repercussions on snow leopard and Tibetan wolf conservation programmes that area NGOs work on.

Hanle has seen the greatest number of attacks by free-ranging dogs on wildlife, livestock and people. Sonam and other locals have been keeping an eye on a pack of six to eight dogs that hunt in the bowl, particularly during the three nesting months of the black-necked cranes, birds sacred to Buddhists. Also under threat from free-ranging dogs are other ground-nesting birds such as the bar-headed goose, the highest-flying migratory bird in the world, which traditionally breeds near the Tso Moriri and a couple of smaller lakes in the Changthang region.

The problem with free-ranging dogs is not particular to Ladakh. A few months prior, I'd seen a dark shape cleave the Beas river in Punjab, leaving a long trail in its wake. From the way it moved, it was neither a human, nor fish, or even a river dolphin. The shape swam with confidence, shrugging off the strong current. It held its line and made straight for a sandbar, hauling itself up on a buff-coloured spit.

It was a black dog, probably free-ranging, but subsidized by any number of villages by the river's edge. It shook itself free of water and, running across the sand, began tugging at the beached carcass of a cow. Another, bigger, dog appeared out of nowhere, and the two began to snarl and gorge, yanking and tearing flesh off the arcing ribs.

River sandbars contain multitudes. The critically endangered gharial, the fish-eating, long-snouted crocodilian, of which no more than a few hundred survive in the world, bask and nest on sandbars. Freshwater turtles like the red-crowned roofed turtle and the Indian narrow-headed soft-shell turtle, among the most endangered of freshwater species, use sand islands extensively to breed and to bask. Hundreds of thousands of birds – some transient visitors from China and Siberia and Central Asia wintering in India, some resident – forage, nest, breed and raise chicks on sandbars. The smooth-clawed river otter and other species raise their pups in riparian mudbank dens, and teach the youngsters to swim and hunt in the area close to riverbanks. Many of these creatures have this in common – to a greater or lesser degree, they are all endangered.

Elsewhere in India, dogs threaten green sea turtles and Olive Ridley turtles which come ashore to nest on the beaches all along the coastline. The critically endangered great Indian bustard in the Thar desert, the blackbuck in the grasslands of the Deccan peninsula and the Asiatic wild ass in the Great Rann of Kutch have been victims of documented attacks by feral dogs. This is by no means an exhaustive list. Dogs compete over carcasses with other predators like jackals and foxes, and with scavenging birds like the critically endangered vultures. Dogs have been responsible for nearly 29 per cent of the foxes found dead in India. Moreover, due to the sheer density of dogs and their ability to range widely, smaller carnivores react to them as they would to a dominant carnivore, depressing food intake by as much as 70 per cent and increasing their vigilance – all signs of stressed behaviour.

Dogs threaten 188 species worldwide, and have effected eleven vertebrate extinctions. India has approximately sixty million dogs, the fourth highest worldwide, and the number is still growing. The scale of the problem is immense. Then there is disease. Distempers and rabies have been known to pass from free-ranging dogs into wild canids. There is also the issue of zoonosis, with the danger of the rabid canids biting humans and passing the disease on. There have been incidences of both in the Changthang region.

'Often, the infected dogs do not have the furious type of rabies,' says Abi Tamim Vanak, who studies wildlife–dog interactions and infectious diseases across India and is a vocal critic of humans subsidizing free-ranging dogs. The classic popular symptoms are not exhibited, and you cannot tell, but the disease is there.

'We humans domesticated dogs,' Vanak explains. 'Dogs came from wolves but, pound for pound, wolves are more powerful. They have bigger jaws and a bone structure that can support a musculature far stronger than that of dogs. Wolves are built for hunting in the wild; they can bring down even large prey easily. Domestic dogs, not so much.'

Dogs cannot survive in the wild without a constant replenishment of their ranks – and free-ranging dogs, Vanak points out, cannot survive without human subsidies. 'Remove human food subsidies,' he says, ticking off the solutions on his fingertips for emphasis. 'Reduce feeding free-ranging dogs in the summer and stop feeding completely in the winter. You will find a drastic reduction in dog population by the following spring.' These are not easy options, they sound inhumane and are challenging to adopt.

In Ladakh, it requires working with the army, which throws away a lot of food that free-ranging dogs gorge on. It also requires the cooperation of tourist camps and of villages all across Ladakh – and here you also run up against the problem of belief systems. Changthang is primarily Buddhist, and Hanle has a number of Tibetan refugee villages. Buddhists believe that dogs come back in their next life as humans. Moreover, being compassionate towards other living beings is ingrained in their religion. So while they want the dogs gone, they are not willing to do what it takes. If they see a hungry dog, they will feed it.

That night in Hanle, we talk into the late hours. The bustle of the nearby camp has died down, the music has stilled. Across the dark skies, the stars sparkle like a million gems embedded in deep velvet. Scorpio ascends the western sky.

A sudden bark shatters the silence. It is answered by another one closer to us. Then another. Now the dogs begin to howl all at once, their echoes bouncing back and forth across the valley in a hellish cacophony.

'Free-ranging dogs need to be reined in,' I recall Vanak's words, as I try for sleep. 'They do not belong in the wild. The wolf does. And we need not reinvent the wolf.'

INTO THE HIDDEN LAND

IN THE TIBETAN PLATEAU NEAR THE NORTHWESTERN TIP OF NEPAL – in proximity to the sacred Mount Kailash, revered as the abode of the Hindu god Shiva – hangs a tongue of the Angsi glacier.

From that tongue flows a trickle of water that bears the name Tamchok Khambab – so christened in the Tibetan holy book Kangri Karchok – which loosely translates to 'the river with a mouth like a horse's ear'. This river is unlike any other on earth.

Cerulean at times, other times emerald, embracing into its fold several different inflows, collecting sediment and gravel along its course, swelling and growing, this river takes on many names, and as many personalities, as it wends its long way home from the high plateau of Tibet to the Bay of Bengal, which borders peninsular India.

By the time it reaches the southern side of the Tibetan capital, Lhasa, the trickle that was the Tamchok Khambab swells to become the Yarlung Tsangpo, 'The Great River'.[1] It then reappears on the Indian side as the Siang river.

The British botanist Frank Kingdon-Ward, who travelled in this region in 1926, was astounded by what he saw. In his book *The Riddle of Tsangpo Gorge*, he says, 'Everywhere, by cliff and rock and scree, by torn scar and ragged rent, wherever vegetation could get and keep a grip, trees grew; and so, from the grinding boulders in the river-bed to the grating glaciers above, the gorge was filled with forest to the very brim.'

The thickly forested gorge that stretches from Kongpo in TAR to Arunachal Pradesh in India is Pemakö – the most famous of the Tibetan Buddhist hidden lands, or *beyul.* Guru Padmasambhava (Guru Rinpoche), who is credited with introducing Tantric Buddhism to Tibet in the eighth century, concealed these locations in his lifetime and decreed that they could only be revealed to Tibetan Buddhists fleeing from political strife and seeking sanctuary. He further proclaimed that only the one who was worthy could 'reveal' such a hidden land and make it accessible to those in need.

In the 1800s, the Great Game played out on the chessboard of Central Asia and Tibet for control of this strategic region. The Russian tsar moved in from the north; the British Raj countered from the south. Threatened from both sides, the Qing emperor in China sealed the 2,400-kilometre border of Tibet in 1850. In 1910, the Qing official Zhao Erfeng, whose ruthlessness earned him the sobriquet 'Zhao the Butcher', invaded eastern and central Tibet and unleashed hellish violence on the Khampas, residents of the Kham region.

This was precisely what Guru Rinpoche had provided for. And in accordance with his decree, the one who was 'worthy' arrived in the form of Dudjom Drakgnak Lingpa, a tertön – revealer of treasures – who made accessible and inhabitable for the oppressed people of the Kham region the previously hidden land of Pemakö. 'The upper end of the valley,' Lingpa wrote in his guide, 'is steep and narrow, while its lower end is wide. The mountain peaks and valleys together form the petals of an open lotus, and the sound of the river's rushing waters can be heard constantly.'

Here, rainbows shone continuously through thick forests full of medicinal plants, and crops grew in abundance. Most importantly, this *beyul* was indestructible. 'No hostile forces,' writes Lingpa, 'can destroy this fortress-like valley. It is the incomparable Enjoyment Body, Sambhogakāya, the outer, inner and most secret supreme realm.'

It was in this fabled region, straddling India's border with China's TAR, that the fleeing Khampas, known in India as Khambas, settled and, in time, grew into what is now among the largest ethnic groups in the lower Pemakö region.

This sacred landscape is considered to be the geographical manifestation of the sow-headed Tibetan goddess of wisdom, queen of the Dakinis – the embodiment of wisdom and energy in female form, who also goes by the names Vajravarahi or Dorje Phagmo. Her five chakras – head, throat, heart, navel and secret – lie on the border of India and Tibet, along the Tsangpo-Siang river basin.

The lofty peak of Kangri Karpo in the TAR manifests as the goddess's head; the peaks of Namche Barwa and Gyala Pelri, both on the Chinese side of the border, are her breasts. The lower chakras lie on the Indian side of the border. Here, nestling within the holy mountain of Devakota, is the sacred womb of the goddess. A tributary of the Siang, known as the Yang Sang Chu or 'Secret River', runs alongside; its waters are said to possess the five wisdoms. And finally, her secret chakra is at the confluence of the tributary Yang Sang Chu and the main stem of the Siang, on the Indian side.

It is the cusp of spring when I reach the lower plains of Assam. With my friend and guide Katon for company, I wind my way up the Siang valley and climb east into the beyul of lower Pemakö, deep in the valley of the 'secret river'. I first heard about this little river eight years ago; since then, it has exercised an inexplicable pull on my imagination. I pored over maps to trace its course from the point of origin to where it joins the Siang, and I read all available literature about it. On the map, the river in mid-course bent around a mountain, almost circumambulating it as if it was doing a *kora*. This mountain – the sacred Devakota – is believed to be the seat of Guru Rinpoche and the womb of the goddess Vajravarahi.

On previous trips up this valley, I only made it as far as the confluence of the Yang Sang Chu, the 'secret river' and the Siang. True to its name, the Yang Sang Chu flows so far below, deep in the bowels of the forested gorge, that there are few places where you can actually see anything more than a rush of rapids before it disappears under an overhang or around a bend. This time, I intend to push deeper into the river valley.

Katon and I make our way up through the Siang valley towards the Chinese border. As the road bends around a mountain, a black eagle soars into view at eye level. Her six-foot wingspan traces wide clockwise spirals; she then banks anti-clockwise, her primary feathers outstretched like fingers. Her head, tucked tight between her wings, is angled down as she intently scans the fog-shrouded floor of the valley, nestling at the foot of steeply sloping montane forests of false hemp trees, East Indian almond, white-boled Canariums flushed red, silk-cotton trees exploding red with inflorescence, magnolias and dipterocarps.

Poking out at regular intervals between these semi-evergreen trees are ancient tree ferns that predate dinosaurs, having evolved 320 million years ago. The velvet worm, the first creature believed to have colonized land, was found to live under these tree ferns, but no scientist has looked for it in over a century. These ancient ferns, thickly knitted in shades of green, are occasionally interrupted by small patches of cultivated clearings that gleam golden, each one studded in its centre with a little palm leaf–roofed hut on stilts. All of it disappears into the foggy gorge, some 500 to 700 metres deep.

Katon shuts off the engine, and we sit in the parked car, watching the raptor as she catches a thermal and rises upwards. The late-winter sun glints off her back; for a brief moment she glows golden, then disappears behind a massive ficus tree. The sun burns the fog away in lifting wisps to reveal the Siang, here coloured teal, sloshing past boulders and around river rocks on its way down to the plains. I thrill to a sight I never tire of seeing.

'Siang is a contraction of Adi words,' says Katon. Asi in Adi means 'water' and àpì-ang means 'heart'. Si-ang, in the language of the Adi people who inhabit this valley, means 'the river that flows through our heart'. The Adi are a fierce and valiant animist tribe of the Siang valley, famed for having beaten back three British 'abor expeditions'. 'Abor' is Assamese for 'savage'; the Adi clans living in the villages dotting the Siang basin earned that moniker for the ruthlessness with which they killed intruding foreigners perceived as hostile. The colonial occupiers of India, even with their advanced weaponry and warcraft, found this region impenetrable in the late-nineteenth and early-twentieth centuries.

Katon leans forward, peering up at an overhang of rock capping a steep cliff rise above us. 'Here is where the Adis stopped the British,' he says, voice edged with pride. 'They built these rock chutes: large baskets of rocks held up by cane ropes tied to trees.' He cups his hand to demonstrate. When the marching column of British sepoys and officers advanced to an area just below the overhang, an Adi positioned on the opposite hill gave the signal; a village elder waiting on the overhang snapped the rope and rocks cascaded out of the basket and down onto the marching column to devastating effect. 'It was my granduncle who cut the rope once,' Katon says. 'It stopped the Britishers; survivors shot him as he fled. He fell to his death – but he had snuffed out the invasion.'

Katon straddles two very different worlds. He is half Adi, and part Khamba, the Tibetan Buddhist warrior clan that migrated south from Tibet in the early 1900s, fleeing persecution.

We halt for the night on the outskirts of the town of Damro, in the Yamne river valley. The Yamne is another of Siang's tributaries, flowing through richly biodiverse terrain that plays host to various Adi clans. Old-growth, impregnable forests crowd the stacked mountain ranges. Panikheti terraces, which divert small mountain streams into fields for growing rice, spread out near the valley floor. Contrasting with this is the rain-fed *jhum kheti*. This type of cultivation, on vertiginous seventy- to eighty-degree inclines, moves every few years as soil becomes less fertile, and shifts back as the fallow soil regains fecundity.

Life here seems untouched by the passage of centuries; I feel as if I have dropped down a rabbit hole into an earlier, elemental age. Adi hunters effortlessly scale 4,000-metre peaks, up beyond the tree line, to hunt for meat and also to harvest the aconite plant, which provides a deadly poison for their arrows. Children tumble down grass and mud slopes on sleds made of bamboo, with little round wooden wheels. Women pound the pith of a sago palm in a large, inverted wooden cone mortar for flour. Men mend their bamboo traps to hunt squirrels and birds in the forest. Families collect medicinal plants to make the starter cake for the ubiquitous local rice brew, apong. They forage for mushrooms in the forests above the villages and join in hunts for the free-roaming *Bos frontalis*, a large, semi-domesticated, bison-like cattle that the locals call 'mithun'.

A day later, Katon and I make the trip up to lower Pemakö, and the confluence of the Siang and Yang Sang Chu. It takes us half a day by car. 'Road' is a misnomer for the route we take. Mountainsides are being clawed and chewed up to create wider roads, and the resultant landslips are an obstacle course we must navigate. His brothers have informed Katon that the road construction has begun to gnaw into lower Pemakö itself. Age-old hanging bamboo bridges, the traditional walking paths of travellers, hunters and pilgrims, have fallen into disrepair. Our original idea of walking for three days in the lower Pemakö region are shelved; we end up with sore backsides from half a day of bumping along on a rocky 'road'.

As we near lower Pemakö, it is not merely the landscape that changes, but life itself. Here, no one recognizes the Adi name 'Katon' – my friend introduces himself as Pema, a Khamba name he uses when he visits the region that supports half his identity. Here, everyone speaks either of two Tibetan dialects, Memba and Khamba; Katon speaks fluent Khamba when he visits. Save for a few far-flung hamlets and gompas, lower Pemakö is all jungle and high peaks of snow. There is no electricity in the valley, no phone network.

Swarms of bloodsucking black flies called *damdims* get to work; their bite makes the blood spill from open wounds. I try in vain to flick them off, while keeping a wary eye out for leeches. There are gongs, prayer beads and wheels, lamas, chanting and drums everywhere – and above it all, the pervasive sound of the gushing waters of the 'secret river', the Yang Sang Chu, flowing below in the gorge.

It has rained all night, and in the indigo of predawn, the lotus valley and the womb of the goddess are shrouded from view. Mist rises and falls and rises again. It is as if the sun has forgotten to show itself. The clouds bulge and burst; thick drops pelt the ground. Katon – now Pema – makes a snap decision. 'Let's go anyway,' he says. The idea is to climb down about 600 metres from our perch at 1,375 metres to the valley floor and then up the holy mountain of Devakota for the kora, a clockwise circumambulation that pilgrims make around holy places and structures.

Devakota for the Buddhists is the 'Deathless Extreme Secret Place' of Guru Rinpoche's prophecy and promise – the womb where the 'seeds of humanity will regenerate themselves after being extinguished at the end of a Dark Age'. When famines and epidemics and wars and violence prevail at the hands of the 'enemies of Dharma', it is said, this wellspring of life which resides at the top of Devakota, under the throne of Guru Rinpoche, will regenerate and renew the world.

We shoulder our backpacks and set off. The damdims are everywhere; their anti-coagulating bite has my blood flowing freely from my hands and other exposed parts of my body. Pema laughs at my plight – the black flies don't bother him, he says; he's grown up with them. He tells me of times when he climbed to the three high sacred spaces in lower Pemakö, among the now-hidden snow mountains, where the rock faces are so sheer they 'are in your nose'; where leeches attack your eyes; wild boars charge from the undergrowth of banana groves, Asiatic black bears scalp heads, tigers walk on pilgrim paths, and vipers litter the humus. The hidden lands are hard to negotiate by design, he tells me; the ancient prophecy decrees that only the pure of intent and the truly devoted will make it there and endure. And yet, the Khambas, Membas and other Tibetan Buddhist sects keep coming to Pemakö, drawn by Dharma and the Promised Land.

As I trudge up the slope of the Devakota, my feet constantly slip and slide, the conditions underfoot made treacherous by rain. Each slip, each slide, sets my heart hammering – the path nudges along narrow ledges that drop precipitously into the Yang Sang Chu gorge. My clothes are sodden, my skin is soaked, the rain keeps pelting down.

We are deep within the heart of the Buddhist belief system. A single kora or circumambulation around Devakota can bestow on the seeker ten billion *siddhis* – unusual skills and powers, unimaginable yogic advancement. To drink the holy water seeping through the mountain is to extend one's life by twenty years. To meditate one day on the holy mountain is equal to meditating for one year anywhere else on earth. This mountain, it is believed, is where the three holiest peaks – Tsetapuri to the north, Riwo Tala to the south, and Pema Shelri to the east – concentrate their sacred energies. For Tibetan Buddhists, the blessings of Guru Rinpoche are worth the gruelling trek with its multitudinous dangers.

To lean over the side of the hanging bridge across the Yang Sang Chu and peer through the prayer flags towards the forests beyond is to allow hundreds of years of faith and history and old-growth nature wash over you. The little 'secret river', ever in a hurry, rushes around Devakota en route to its meeting with the Siang. Mist, like the very breath of the gods, rises from thickly knitted canopies. Rocks are swaddled in moss mats an inch thick and dripping with moisture. I cup my hands beneath one and drink the water that drips into my palms. It is sweet and cold and life-giving.

Loopy, twisted, woody vines – lianas – shrouded in lichen and ferns, fungi and orchids festoon the understory of the forest. Deep, hollow burrows tell of a time when bears hibernated. Prayer flags of devotees who have trekked here over the years hang on every bamboo handrail and twisted cane wire, some so old they are now lichen-and-fungus flags. The warm aroma of humus and lignin combine with incense, lit at a chorten. Caves here are believed to be the home of spirits and goddesses. Peering down from a high ledge, I see a rivulet rushing out of a cave and flowing down to join the Yang Sang Chu. Such caves are believed to exude *sindura*, the sacred menstrual flow of the goddess of wisdom.

Faith and fable, devotion and a sense of destiny hang suspended in the air around us; the power of this place, infused with centuries of belief, is strong enough to cradle, and revive, the weariest of pilgrims who seek to circumambulate the womb of the goddess.

At the top of the Devakota nestles a tiny monastery. I walk into the single chamber within and instinctively prostrate before the large golden statue of a seated Guru Rinpoche. As prescribed, I raise my hands, palms touching, above my head. I rise to my knees, palms together in front of my chest, and I ask for blessings for all creatures on earth. I get up and raise my hands again, and fall to my knees once more, this time seeking blessings for my family. I stand up a third time and raise my hands high above my head, then drop to my knees – and suddenly, unaccountably, the tears come.

I weep, my breath coming in sharp, short intakes that echo around the walls of the monastery. A lama seated under the gong stops chanting momentarily to look at me. My knees give way; I sink to the floor and lean against an ornate carved pillar. A ginger cat that enthusiastically welcomed us at the top of the mountain crawls into my lap and licks my face. In this place, within the force field of holy mountains that for centuries has attracted the devout from all across the Buddhist world, my worldliness evaporates. In that moment I am stripped of pretence; I feel like I am nothing, and everything, all at once.

Precious places are by definition fragile, and Pemakö is no exception. If China's recent five-year plan comes to fruition, it will bring new danger to this land. It won't be long before loud rumblings of heavy machinery and the thunder of blasting reverberate in upper Pemakö, announcing China's largest hydropower dam, where the Tsangpo falls 6,500 feet to morph into the Siang. This activity, in the name of development, is deadly in a region where the mountains are young and still thrusting upwards: since 1600, most of the largest earthquakes have occurred in the last 120 years. Moreover, any dam built upstream by China means denial of water and vital sediments to India, midstream, and to Bangladesh, in the lower basin. And all of this is not counting the potential damage to the ecologically fragile hidden lands of the Pemakö, a repository of Buddhist tradition and culture.

An environmental conflict looms as India, in a bid to stake first claim to the waters of the Tsangpo and subvert Chinese plans, firms up its intent to build its own dams in the valleys of Arunachal Pradesh. The sites have been identified; when construction begins, vital old-growth forests, towns, hamlets and whole swathes of indigenous sacred lands and cultures will be submerged.

The site of the secret *chakra* of the goddess of wisdom, where the Yang Sang Chu meets the Siang, already bristles with tractors and JCBs. India is building a highway across the sacred confluence and down the spine of the Siang valley. Road-cutting machinery chomps the mountainsides on both sides of the border, their incessant whine drowning out the rutting of deer and the call of the whistling thrushes in the forests above. The surge of conflicting emotions induced by my kora and the perceived sacrilege of ill-conceived infrastructure planning clash in my mind.

I have watched Katon go seamlessly from an Adi skipping sideways on uneven rocks by the Siang to Pema, the Khamba, moving through the thick stands of old forest, at ease on slippery slopes – both avatars knowing where a bear has paused or which berry is inedible. I have marvelled as he swam against a current in a rushing river and lit wood that was dripping with rain; I've been awestruck by the sight of him hauling forty kilograms up a sixty-degree incline and hacking his way through a stubborn knot of undergrowth.

Katon, in his element, contrasts starkly with young Adi and Khamba students I have met in towns, their heads constantly bent over their phones, their faces lit by the glow of the little screen, their lives and minds and hearts entirely divorced from their ancestral wildlands.

I recall a line from Aldo Leopold's *A Sand County Almanac*. 'Civilization,' Leopold writes, 'has so cluttered this elemental man-earth relationship with gadgets and middlemen that awareness of it is growing dim. We fancy that industry supports us, forgetting what supports industry.'

As we make our way around Devakota, completing the kora, trekking up and climbing down over and over again, I trace with my feet the ancient rhythms of this still-beating heart of the Buddhist world. With every step there is a sense of reverence, with every other step a sense of impending loss. I wonder how much longer we have before this hidden land, too, disappears into the maw of 'progress'.

PART 5

THE SOUND OF CITIES

WHERE THE WILD THINGS STILL ARE

I've often thought that if our zoning boards could be put in charge of botanists, of zoologists and geologists, and people who know about the earth, we would have much more wisdom in such planning than we have when we leave it to the engineers.

WILLIAM O. DOUGLAS[1]

Early April 2020

I LIVE IN A GATED COMMUNITY OF INDEPENDENT HOUSES, EACH surrounded by a patch of green and picket-fenced from five neighbours whose walls rise not ten feet away from mine. From my terrace, the view is of neat rows of red-tiled roofs sloping away from us, drawing the eyes towards an array of glass-and-steel buildings – tech parks, the glittering badges of Bangalore's identity as the 'Silicon Valley of India'. These buildings surround us in all directions; life in this gated community is akin to living in a shallow well.

Within this well, the community is laid out like a skeleton, with a black-topped central spine and lanes branching off it in ramrod-straight symmetry. Bottle-shaped palms with smooth boles, alien to our geography, flank the spine and the lanes. It is the builder's version of a desert-oasis settlement, or of California suburbia.

Occasional laments from residents – 'The leaves from the tree keep falling on my car'; 'Can we please plant trees that won't carpet the ground with flowers which will then have to be cleaned?' – have resulted in inappropriate landscaping choices. Brightly coloured invasive bushes which, if left to their own devices, will take over the entire landscape, adorn garden hedges; dark-green topiaries poke out from front yards; incongruous pine trees line garden pathways; traveller palms from Madagascar fan their arms out in wide arcs as if to ask, 'What on earth am I doing here?'; droopy-beaked creepers from South America jostle for attention with the thirsty palms. And then, of course, there is the urban Indian obsession with inert lawns. They are everywhere.

In this manicured community, my messy, overgrown garden is an anomaly. I don't allow the gardener the luxury to express himself with his secateurs. A climbing bamboo, now over twenty-five feet high, threatens to clamber all over the back of my house, its needy tentacles spreading wildly, clutching at air until it finds something to cling to. Native trees – Indian laburnum, moringa, three tall magnolias, a many-branched umbrella tree, a broad-leafed Butea and a mango tree – have grown taller than my villa itself. A lilac Petrea and a madhumalati creeper, unrestricted by garden shears, have blanketed the front of my house.

In this tiny urban wilderness, a seed thick with silky white pappus flew in on the wind, found a home, took root and sprouted. I noticed it only when the plant was about a foot high. The gardener wanted to uproot it – in his worldview, this was a weed with no ornamental value. 'It's common, it grows by the roadside, no one puts it in their gardens!' he wailed, afraid perhaps that his reputation will be degraded if this 'weed' were to flourish in a garden under his watch.

'It will obstruct the view,' he tried. The seed had chosen a spot right under the nose of a four-foot-high bust of the Buddha, a cynosure for visitors, and a 'weed' growing wild in front of it would mar its serene visage. Or so he argued.

'It's a milkweed, a host plant for plain tiger butterflies,' I told him. Moreover, its flowers are deemed sacred; its stem fibre is used as rope; its leaves have medicinal properties. This was a special plant, and uprooting it to satisfy someone's notion of a clean garden was not an option. 'People can peek at the Buddha through its branches.'

Ever since I won the argument, a *Calotropis gigantea* – crown flower in English, *aak* in Hindi, *aakdo* in the deserts of Rajasthan, *ekke gida* in Kannada – has grown, unmolested, to a height of fifteen feet.

I step out onto my terrace with a cup of filter coffee, a pair of binoculars and a camera. I watch a purple-rumped sunbird, brilliant in its attire of magenta necklace, jade green crown, yellow breast and metallic purple rump, hang upside down from a curl of Petrea, stick its tongue into a flower and drink deeply.

Something dark appears in my peripheral field of view. I adjust the focus on my binoculars and draw in a sharp breath: a shiny, bulbous obsidian creature, two inches in length, with huge oblong eyes the colour of turquoise and wings of emerald and sapphire – but wait, are those wings of amethyst and fire … and now they're turned emerald and amethyst … Its colours shift constantly as it moves, as if on a flower-turntable, catching angles of light and refracting it back in myriad hues. As suddenly as it had appeared, it vanishes.

I walk to the edge of the terrace and lean over the parapet, my face close to the shrub. The flower still bobs slightly from the release of its visitor's weight, but the jewelled creature is nowhere to be seen. A deep, resonant buzz makes me turn to my right, and I see the flying wanderer hang briefly in the air, turning its body a full 360 degrees in a look-at-me move. It is close enough now for me to gaze into those startling blue eyes. But all too soon it zooms off in a now-colourless blur of wings.

Drawing back from the edge of the parapet, I squint at the LCD display of my camera. The shifting iridescence – blue, purple, green, ochre – in its wings is stunning. Later that day, I post the photo to Twitter, mistakenly calling the wondrous creature a bumblebee.

'It's a carpenter bee,' a wildlife biologist corrects me. The only bumblebees in India are found in the Himalaya, I am reminded. And thus begins my journey into a beguiling lesser-known world – the world of solitary bees, not least the carpenter bee, genus Xylocopa.

One of the best-kept secrets of the bee world is this: of the 20,400 species in the world, over 90 per cent do not live in hives, nor do they make any honey. That percentage soars in India where, of the 700 or so bee species, only five are social bees, living in hives and producing honey. The rest are 'solitary' – there is no 'queen bee' being served by 'worker bees', no social hierarchy. These bees live independently, foraging and fending for themselves. And in doing so, they play an important role in our world. Solitary bees are crucial to the successful pollination of several crops such as cucurbits, blueberry, cranberry, tomatoes, eggplants, apples, plums, almonds, and all manner of lentils.

Bees have always found a special place in the human imagination. Bhramari in Hindu mythology is a bee goddess, an incarnation of goddess Parvati, the consort of Lord Shiva. Legend has it that Parvati commands all the bees, wasps and flies of the world, which cling to her body, and she assumes the avatar of Bhramari in battle against the demon Arunasura. The demon, invincible by virtue of boons received in return for his penance, is nevertheless vanquished when hordes of bees and wasps leave Bhramari's body at her command and attack him.

The big, black, shiny carpenter bee, the *bhramara*, appears often in Sanskrit poetry, usually hovering around young maidens as a proxy for lovesick men. In a famous incident from the Hindu epic Mahabharata, Karna, who at the time is training under Parasurama, is stung by a large bee (presumably a female carpenter bee as males do not carry stings) but does not flinch, as his guru's head is resting on his lap and any sudden movement would disturb his sleep. On waking and seeing Karna's bleeding thigh and noting his stoic forbearance, Parasurama realizes that his disciple must be a Kshatriya (warrior), for no one else could have borne such pain. This was a detail that Karna had misrepresented to his guru. Parasurama, famed for his temper, flies into a rage and curses Karna, a curse that proves to be the warrior's undoing in his final battle against Arjuna.

Records suggest that these big bees were used to carry messages tied to their thorax,[2] much in the same way as carrier pigeons were historically employed. Carpenter bees are also supposed to be great at trap-lining, with individual bees following set routes to forage for food. These bees remember and recognize food plants and flowers and can easily find their way back to the same area every time. It's no wonder that they doubled up as messenger bees for their human keepers. Thieves kept carpenter bees in boxes and released them after sundown into houses, where they promptly extinguished lamps, making thievery more feasible.

Aside from one social honeybee species, *Apis mellifera*, introduced into our ecosystem, all the bees found in India, both solitary and social, are natives. And of these natives, the one I've just caught foraging on my terrace is the largest – the female *Xylocopa latipes*.

Intrigued, I begin to consciously seek out bees in my overgrown urban garden, where I have made room for mostly native flowering plants. Over time, I notice that at least four species of carpenter bees come each day, and several other species of solitary bees visit occasionally.

The signs are everywhere: neatly cut-out laminae of leaves tell of leaf-cutter bees; eyes stare out from thin hollow sticks and wall crevices, bearing testimony to the roosting place of the fuzzy-thoraxed woolly wall bee (a type of mason bee). Once I start looking, bees with abdomens banded blue and green, some black and yellow, others polka-dotted blue and black are everywhere.

Only three of the many species of bees in my garden turn out to be honeybees. The largest is the giant Indian honeybee or rock bee, *Apis dorsata*, while the dwarf bee, *Apis florea*, is the smallest. The third – *Apis cerana* – is neither too big nor too small. Peering into the foliage of Petrea one day, I find a dwarf honeybee hive, from which these tiny bees venture out to forage for nectar and pollen on Petrea and moringa flowers. These bees seem to be partial to a nearby patch of basil. I realize, to my astonishment, that all the other bees I spot in my garden are solitary bees – and to think we go through life assuming all bees live in hives!

Each morning, as the summer sun comes up, the carpenter bees appear. They follow a pattern – one species, usually the fluffy yellow *Xylocopa pubescens*, is the first to arrive, the male leading the way. The female, sporting a yellow thorax and black abdomen like a mini taxicab, follows. As she climbs to the soundtrack of their buzzing, other species zoom in from various directions.

The last to visit, announcing her arrival from afar with a loud buzz of wings beating over 100 times a second, thereby carrying along with her a miniature weather system of swirling air, is the massive *Xylocopa latipes*, the world's second largest.

Oftentimes her legs or the underside of her abdomen will be covered in yellow pollen that adheres to her as she goes about collecting nectar; it is this pollen she will then unwittingly deposit on the next plant she visits, thus assisting in pollination even as she provisions for her next generation.

The female carpenter bees carries nectar in their bellies, and pollen on their legs and on the undersides of their abdomen. When fully laden, she zooms away, most likely to a large, dried bamboo pole that she would have chewed a circular hole in. The hollow chamber between two nodes is her nest; within that chamber she would have created several compartments, one for each egg she will eventually deposit.

When she returns to her nest, she regurgitates the nectar and mixes it with pollen to fashion 'bee bread', a food high in protein and calories. This she deposits in one compartment, lays a single egg there and seals it. She repeats the process in the next compartment, and then the next, until the hollow bamboo chamber is filled.

Something even more interesting takes place in the topmost chamber in their nest. The egg laid in that chamber usually hatches a male. Breaking out of the topmost chamber, the male prepares to mate with the females of the generation. How mother bees engineer this perfect system is still not fully understood.

The bee bread the female bee deposits in each compartment serves as food for the larva that will emerge. It will eat, pupate and emerge as a bee, making its way out of the chamber to mate, provision and carry on the lineage. The mother will, in all likelihood, never meet the offspring of her offspring, for these species are solitary in more ways than one.

Nesting sites are key to the survival of these species. Solitary bees tend to live separately, with only the female building a nest. Sometimes females will build burrows, or bore holes close to one another, but rarely do such bees share nests. The males find grasses or other surfaces to hold on to, or little depressions to sleep in at night – they do not build or use nests. Carpenter bees, as their name suggests, carve holes into wood or bamboo with their powerful mandibles. Others, like mason bees, blue-banded bees and leaf-cutter bees burrow into mud or nest in small cavities.

During the process of urbanization, mud, bamboo, wood and other permeable surfaces are the first to be paved over or clear-cut, replaced by tarmac, tiles and concrete. This results in fewer nesting sites for solitary bees. While these bees are generalists and can manage well in urban gardens, it is the availability of nesting sites that determines the health of their population. A decrease in nesting sites is one of the strongest indicators that there will be a decline in species biodiversity.

'We have shown that in pigeon pea (*toor dal*, in Hindi) plots, if you increase nesting sites, you can almost double the pod set,' says Dr Belavadi, a pollination biologist. While the pigeon pea can self-pollinate – that is, produce pod sets without the aid of an external pollinator – the yield is only 18–20 per cent in such cases. If left open to pollinate, without any help to the pollinators, the yield rises to 30–35 per cent. But if leaf-cutter bees are provided additional nesting sites like hollow reeds, pipes or bamboos, close to pigeon pea plots, the yield jumps to 50–60 per cent.

Some important crop plants like chillies, bell peppers and tomatoes need to be 'buzz-pollinated'. The anthers in such flowers require a certain amount of vibration in order to release pollen. The exact mechanism of release is still being studied, but that bees play an important role in providing this vibration through their wingbeat frequency is key.

Far more than honeybees, solitary bees are efficient at buzz pollination. Increasing nesting sites for solitary bees around farms where such crops are grown is therefore known to be beneficial. This holds true for urban and peri-urban farms, as also for kitchen and terrace gardens. Studies have also shown spillover effects where rural agricultural land that borders urban spaces are aided by a high incidence of pollinators in the urban areas.[3]

While Indian data on the subject is scarce, in certain other parts of the world, parallels have been drawn between the health of pollinator (specifically bee) populations and species biodiversity in natural and semi-natural areas with urban sprawl, manicured urban gardens, dense concrete cities, rural sites of intensive agriculture, and urban and rural commons.

The results are instructive and illuminating for city planners and residents alike, pointing to distinct strategies for increasing pollinator diversity and protecting bee populations.

It is well known that native bee diversity is most adversely affected in areas of intense monoculture agriculture where the use of pesticides and chemicals is heavy. These landscapes here tend to be resource-poor. Dense urbanization with a high degree of impermeable surfaces like concrete and glass, tarmac and tiles restrict nesting sites severely. Close-packed high-rise buildings fragment food resource connectivity and put dense built-up urban spaces second from the bottom in bee diversity and pollinator health.

The kinds of flora urban spaces afford bees is important too. Most urban areas tend to be dominated by generalist species of solitary bees, happy to forage on exotic plants. But this crowds out species that have a narrower foraging strategy which may very well have been satisfied in natural or semi-natural spaces with a high biodiversity of native flora. This also works the other way around – when pollinators that prefer certain host plants or native species are edged out, exotic or invasive species take over the urban landscapes.

Urbanization has also brought with it the heat-island effect. When trees that line our roads are chopped down, the ambient air temperature increases by 3.5°Celsius and the surface temperature of the tarmac shoots up by 25–30°Celsius. By the end of the century, our cities could be seven degrees hotter.

Such temperature changes favour species that prefer warmth while foraging. They take to warmer micro-habitats like city centres, which may be rich in food resources by way of ornamental flowers, while bee species that prefer cooler temperatures are likely to be pushed out to the outskirts, areas that may not be as rich in food sources. The effect of light, noise, air pollution and climate change on solitary bee biodiversity needs far more research but broadly, generalists tend to do better when the going gets tough, while specialists or species that rely on a narrow range of food resources, or on certain native species of flora, tend to suffer.

July 2020

Ever since that day in April 2020, when I zoomed into the world of solitary bees, I have been documenting their behaviour. Now, I see and hear these creatures everywhere. Any time I spy a dead bejewelled bee, I pick it up and peer at it through a magnifying glass. I collect shiny chitinous parts and assorted wings. It becomes a joke in the house. 'There goes Mamma again, collecting dead insects,' my daughter groans. She'd been startled when a box of chocolates, eagerly opened, was found to contain long-dead bees, one in each little depression.

I shoot videos and send it to researchers like Dr Hema Somanathan, a plant-pollinator researcher in IISER, Thiruvananthapuram, who patiently translates the significance of the bee-behavior I have recorded. Through extensive lockdown conversations on the phone and through WhatsApp, she progressively opens doors for me into the bee-world. I read obsessively, and bees – solitary bees in particular – become my obsession.

One morning I wake up to a pungent, suffocating smell. The nationwide lockdown, imposed abruptly in March 2020, has been relaxed, and the gardeners are back. Someone, somewhere in my lane, has sprayed a stinking pesticide. I put on my mask and step out; my nose leads me to the offending garden. The gardener has left. A quick phone call determines that he has used banned broad-spectrum pesticides on the lawn. The impact is immediate and visible: a resident elsewhere in the community complains of finding dead bees and various kinds of insects in his garden.

A few more phone calls throw up names of deadly chemicals – chlorpyrifos, phorate – that have been used liberally by the returning gardeners. The community rallies around and agrees to prohibit these killer chemicals from entering our gardens.

Within our community, the problem is quickly identified, and easily resolved. But in our cities it looms large. Urban India, with its great affinity for lawns, still uses broad-spectrum insecticides – organophosphates like phorates and neonicotinoids, among others, which are banned in Western countries. These chemicals are known to affect honeybee populations, if not many others. How they affect solitary bees and, consequently, the fauna that prey on them is not known, but can be inferred from the devastation they have caused to honeybee colonies. In addition, when seeds are treated with pesticides, the residual toxicity finds its way into the pollen. These residues have been implicated in colony collapse disorders in the US, a predicament yet to be studied in India.

But there is hope for our cities, and our solitary bees. Urbanization per se does not mean lowered solitary bee biodiversity. In fact, urban sprawl, with a green corridor that leads in from the rural or natural landscape up to the city centre, could foster a high degree of it if only urban planners and landscapers would build cities with adequate food resources and ground- and cavity-nesting sites for pollinators in mind.

The difference residents can make is significant too. Dr Somanathan, my bee-guru and Xylocopa-guide, urges urbanites to build 'bee hotels' and host solitary bees. 'All it takes is some hollow wooden sticks or bamboo tied together and hung for the cavity-nesting species, and some soil left free in gardens, rather than paved or tiled over, for the ground-nesting species,' she says.

I imagine a world where we don't use any harmful chemicals. We let wildflowers bloom, we plant vines of pumpkins and tomatoes and wild milkweed and create little havens for solitary bees. They get their nectar and pollen, and we get fruits and vegetables and flowers. How can this not be the way forward?

Dr Somanathan's strategy is playing out in my terrace garden. Almost every segment of bamboo – and I have plenty of bamboo – betrays a neat round hole made by a female carpenter bee. I see pollen stuck at every doorstep, telltale signs of a squeeze into that hole after a successful foraging trip. I've seen leaf-cutter bees and mason bees huddle in frangipani branch hollows, while honeybees visit the cilantro and basil patches every morning.

The city of Bangalore, ballooning as it is, still has pockets of reprieve for its wild denizens. For several centuries, rulers of the area recognized the need for its water security and built several water structures. A number of connected man-made lakes, upstream to downstream, provide water to the citizens. Some date back to the sixteenth century and the reign of Kempe Gowda I, a chieftain of the Vijayanagara Empire and ruler of Yelahanka. Others are even older. Almost all are hotspots for bird life and smaller, lesser noticed but equally important, wildlife.

The biggest lake in Bangalore is Bellandur Lake, directly northwest of where I live. It dates back to the fifth century, which saw the reign of the Western Ganga Dynasty. Sadly it is the one of the most polluted lakes in the city today, frothing with sewage and effluents that are pumped into it from the settlements and industries on its banks. Several other lakes in Bangalore are in varying stages of death and decay, while a few have been resurrected by residents' associations and the sheer willpower of a few individuals.

All these lakes support birds, fish, odonates (dragonflies and damselflies), bats, mongooses, snakes and all manner of other insects. The stench of methane emanating from the dirtier lakes makes one gag; the sight of a stoic heron standing knee-deep in dark muck, gulping down a fish evokes despair. At a nearby pond, a heron rocking on hyacinth, its white feathers dark from filthy waters, only intensifies that feeling. At some remove, however, the stench fades. Saul Kere, a short walk to the west of the glass-and-concrete well I live in, is a smaller and somewhat cleaner lake where hundreds of species of birds have been recorded across seasons.

Dr Belavadi is doggedly positive: 'I still consider a city like Bangalore, with its 500 or so parks, and its lakes and thousands of home-gardens, the Garden City,' he says. 'We have a great opportunity to protect our solitary bee biodiversity.'

Late September 2020

The southwest monsoon is spent and has all but retreated. I am on my terrace just in time to catch a huge flock of ibises heading southwest. I count over fifty. They fly in a V formation, shuffle positions occasionally into a straight line, rearranging themselves into a V again, as they head off into the sunset. They are possibly going from one Bangalore lake to another. A few minutes later, another curve of sixty ibises – too far for me to tell if they are the same species – flies the same route. And all this time, the sky is changing hues.

As a purple-pink twilight fades to obsidian, a never-ending river of flying foxes – the largest fruit bat in India – flows overhead from their roosting site somewhere to my west, heading east.

I turn to see two female carpenter bees, probably sisters from a previous brood, return home to bake some pollen-and-nectar bee bread. I watch, grinning like the Cheshire Cat and hugging myself in glee, as they hover over neat circular holes in the bamboos, unwittingly dabbing a bit of pollen at their doorstep as they squeeze in headfirst.

LISTENING TO LANDSCAPES

IMAGINE A CIVILIZATION, A FEW THOUSAND PEOPLE STRONG, living on a snaking ribbon of a planet 1,600 kilometres long, with steep drop-offs on either side. The atmosphere above is rich with oxygen, but only thirty feet thick on average. Women, men, children are productive, industrious, educated and able. They are also all blind. They communicate aurally, using elaborate and sophisticated sound signatures. Different frequencies are employed to fulfil needs: from foraging for food to socializing, from finding friends and mates to detecting danger, from protecting oneself to rearing children. Some tasks are accomplished using very low frequencies, while others require high frequencies. Nothing can be accomplished without sound.

One day, suddenly, the airspace above this land is invaded by drones. They fly low, high, fast, slow; they buzz, beep, rumble, wheeze. Propellers cut into the airspace above the heads of the men, women, children. The blind people try to raise their voices to be heard above the din. They try to shift their communication frequencies so as to find food, meet friends, talk to their children. This requires the expenditure of considerable energy, and the effort tires them out.

Their efforts to adapt, to find new frequencies through which to communicate, are futile as the ambient sound spans a wide range of frequencies and drowns out everything from a whisper to a scream. The denizens try to move, but the drones are everywhere, their noise all-pervasive.

Finding food becomes impossible. Social interactions are no longer effective. Alarms sounding danger are silenced, and fatal collisions with propellers of low-flying drones increase. Children cannot hear their parents calling out to them. Connections with friends and mates dwindle. Fewer and fewer people breed successfully. Even those that do can barely secure food to support their families. Squeezed out of their spaces, their numbers drop slowly at first, then drastically, until one day the whole civilization is snuffed out.

What reads like dystopian fantasy is all too real; the world you just read about could be akin to that of India's National Aquatic Animal, the effectively blind Gangetic river dolphin that inhabits the Ganga–Brahmaputra–Meghna river basin. Think of this snaking land as the Ganga, the drones as the ships and barges, cruises, dredgers and trawlers. The anthropogenic sounds emitted and transmitted through the river overpower the high-frequency clicks the river dolphins produce for echolocation, a sound essential for everything from foraging to mating. But the construction of India's National Waterways 1 and 2, which extend up and down the Ganga–Brahmaputra basin, will cover 90 per cent of the cetacean's home range. And the Gangetic dolphin has been suffering metabolic stress resulting from increased acoustic pollution caused by shipping traffic.

Sound has information, it has shape. It is characterized by texture, colour, weight and emotion. Sound triggers memory, it makes us laugh and weep. It can soothe; it can drive us to anger.

Sound is mechanical energy that has a physical impact. Its vibrations – sound waves – travel through the air to the ear, get picked up by aural sensors and translate into what we finally hear. What sound waves do is tap on your eardrum. A strong enough sound can whomp us to the ground. The loudest of sounds can kill us.

Sound is measured in decibels. A whisper measures 20 decibels; normal breathing is 10. But it is a logarithmic scale: a vacuum cleaner at 70 decibels is twice as loud as a restaurant conversation at 60. If you were to subject yourself for eight hours to the juddering of a jackhammer, the revving of a motorcycle, or a farm tractor running at full throttle, you would risk serious damage to your eardrum.

Our ears may recover from a sudden loud sound, but a constant vibration on our eardrums at 80 decibels and more can be downright dangerous, causing lasting damage. In the torture chambers of Abu Ghraib and elsewhere, a preferred method of punishment was to clamp earphones on prisoners' ears, and to blast music at maximum volume.

Walking with Paul Salopek across Punjab, during harvest season, I realize just what such an assault on our aural system can feel like. En route to Abohar, we trek along National Highway 7 – the aorta of agrarian commerce in northwest India – and it provides the percussive underpinning to a soundtrack from hell. Tractors flow past in an endless sequence, the rhythmic thup-thup of their engines offset by the relentless beats of remixed soundtracks, blaring from custom-fitted stereos. A truck overloaded with wheat teeters up the road, its banshee whine a protest against the impossible load it is carrying. A groaning tractor-trailer, bulging with chaff, nudges us off the shoulder of the road. The wall of noise has our nerves jangling and we search for a slice of quietude.

It is so debilitating that we look for pathways much farther away from the main highway. Imagine, though, the driver on his tractor, his ears buffeted by the incessant roar of the engine and the thump of the music beat inches from his ears. Imagine the ceaseless assault on his eardrums. Tractors at full load can reach a decibel level of 120. The music blares over and above that. Prolonged exposure to these levels means damage is immediate and potentially permanent.

Just twenty yards off the blistering highway tarmac, we find trees. Walking twenty yards perpendicular to the highway takes us from the blare of horns to the rustle of wheat, from the whine of overladen trucks to the lowing of indolent cows. Just twenty yards take us from thumping electronic dance music to lilting birdsong. After a few days of the heat, dust and relentless noise of NH7, our longing for the silence of backcountry dirt roads becomes an obsession.

We search for untrafficked, untarmacked back roads. We beseech shopkeepers, farmers, cyclists, hoteliers for walked routes, we scour Google Maps for traces of light white roads which meant no highways, for hints of goat and camel tracks, shepherd paths – anything but tarmac, anything that would take us from torture to tranquillity.

On lucky days when we do come upon such paths, the sand underfoot is fine, yielding willingly beneath our feet, our shoes making a soothing chush-chush as we walk. The lack of noise frees up our attention, our mindspace, to the astounding array of sights and sensations with which the desert teems.

Bangalore, 9:30 a.m.

A truck groans, cars honk, a motorcycle sputters into motion, clothes slap against stone, wood strikes wood, a door bangs shut, a man yells into his phone on the lawn beneath my window, a huge metal clang shatters the air as if something big has fallen from a height, the wind shivers through the palm fronds. A high-pitched whine from a nearby tech park fills the air, drowning the light tapping of my fingers on the keyboard and the musical three-toned coos of a spotted dove.

Anthropogenic sound – often dubbed noise – is changing our world and our lived experience. Noise is the 'ignored pollutant'; it is known to lead to hypertension, anxiety, heart disease and depression.

Building on Canadian philosopher Marshall McLuhan's seminal work on media theory, Nicholas Carr in his book *The Shallows* furthers the argument that when the printing press became ubiquitous and more and more people began to read, our visual acuity sharpened at the expense of our other senses. The shift to reading, he argues, made humans more insular, as reading is primarily a solitary activity. Reading this is likely keeping you from noticing and engaging with your surrounds as you would otherwise, with all five senses.

We have disconnected not only from the natural world but, by cocooning ourselves in a controlled, manufactured space that takes us deeper into our echo chambers and discourages engagement – physical, aural, tactile or olfactory – we have 'othered' Nature. We think of Nature as being elsewhere; it is now a tourist destination we can 'enjoy' on weekends for a few hours of 'detox'. It isn't supposed to always be around us; our relationship with it is now transactional rather than integral.

Walking through landscapes breaks us out of that cocoon. When we walk, sans earphones isolating us from the space we are passing through, we begin to reclaim some of that awareness of our place in the world. We begin to reconnect, listen, feel, smell; we start to belong with our whole being to the community of creatures.

We begin to hear differently. The wind speaks to us in tongues. It blows in soft susurrations through a khejri, but rustles bamboo; it slaps through a magnolia tree but crashes through palms. The wingbeat of a sunbird is a hurried futhurrrr, while that of a spotted dove is a discrete fut-fut-fut-fut-fut, while the great hornbill makes an air-rending, reverberating thwack-thwack-thwack. In contrast, the barn owl defies its size and glides silently through the night. Parakeets fly tipsy, shrieking with every few flaps, careening through the air, while the black kites ride thermals, soaring, circling, rising high: cheee-cheee-cheeeeeeee. The whine of mosquitoes is the sound of sleeplessness, the sound of a bee is all busy-ness. The buzz of a carpenter bee is far louder, and more coherent than the feathery buzz of a honeybee. And among carpenter bees, the deep, bass hmmmmmmmm of an approaching massive *Xylocopa latipes* could readily drown out the zzzz of a furry ochre-coloured *Xylocopa pubescens*.

Rain strikes a tin roof with the percussive power of a rock backbeat, but when it falls on thatch, it is with the whisper of brush on canvas. Early-monsoon raindrops on the Ganga can be mist-like, calling up the fish (remember that Bengali term for this rain that heralds the hilsa-fishing season – ilsheguri brishti), while later in the season, it strikes the river heavily, pocking and welting the jade-green water.

To listen is to step into a fourth dimension of the world around us.

Sound, by its absence, too, makes its mark.

> I do not know which to prefer,
> The beauty of inflections
> Or the beauty of innuendoes,
> The blackbird whistling
> Or just after.
>
> WALLACE STEVENS,
> 'Thirteen Ways of Looking at a Blackbird'[1]

In December 2011, deep in the jungles of the Pakke Tiger Reserve in Arunachal Pradesh, the District Forest Officer Tana Tapi clears a path for us to the Pakke river, slashing and hacking through the undergrowth with his traditional Nyishi *dao*, the dagger every tribesman carries.

I walk in his wake, trying to ignore each sharp blade of grass that swipes my skin with a swish. At each bend, he motions for me to stop, a finger on his lips. 'Elephants move silently,' he whispers. 'They could be coming towards you, hidden by the bend, and you will not hear them.' His words astound me. Surely a four-tonne fully grown elephant's movements will produce sound!

A year later, in the fall of 2012, the lesson comes home to roost.

A herd of elephants – big, small, male, female, brown, grey – graze on the exposed grassy banks of a tank in central Sri Lanka's

Kalawewa National Park, thickly hemmed in by lofty, leafy Arjuna trees flushed red from the sun. It is the dry season; water sources are evaporating higher in the hills. Substantial man-made tanks, several centuries old, beckon one of the world's largest congregations anywhere of wild Asian elephants.

A constant chizz of cicadas from afar fills the air, punctuated by an occasional trumpet or a low rumble from the pachyderms. Egrets hop eagerly, dodging the tree-trunk-like legs of the elephants, snatching up insects thrown up by huge feet shaking loose clumps of grass.

Two elephants, a mother and her calf, frolic in a ditch of water among the Arjuna trees behind me. I turn to watch them through my binoculars. Suddenly a gunshot rends the air. I swing around to check on the herd but it has vanished.

A hundred elephants, gone.

A short trumpet cues me to turn right, and I find the whole herd running at full tilt in a wide arc all the way into the forest of Arjunas which will eventually make them come up behind me. I see them, I hear their trumpets of alarm, but no noise emerges from their footsteps.

The sound of a hundred elephants – some 400 tonnes of flesh and bones on the move – is indeed the sound of silence.

But Nature can be noisy too. If you ask the decibel meter, the blue whale and the sperm whale are noisier than jet planes at take-off. A snapping shrimp produces a sound that measures 200 decibels underwater, like a gun going off, prompting its nickname – pistol shrimp. Often, the smallest of creatures can be the loudest.

One summer evening, exhausted from fieldwork on the banks of the Ganga in Bihar, I shrug off my camera bag, shower and fall asleep with the lights on in my room. Suddenly, at 1 a.m., I am awakened by what sounds like a shrill fire alarm: kee kee kee kee kee kee kee kee.

In a stupor, I pull on my shoes, pick up my wallet and peep out of the hotel room door, ready to make a run for it. But there is no one in the hallway. Not a soul has stirred, but the noise does not stop. It dawns on me then that the noise is emerging from my own room. Sloughing off the last vestiges of sleep, I follow the sound and finally locate its source sitting smug behind my backpack.

A cricket, not even an inch long, has been stridulating in the dead of night. I crouch to get a better look. Alarmed by what might have seemed like a giant descending beside it, it goes quiet. I do not move. And it starts up again. Rubbing its wings, one on another, a cricket can produce sound that is over 100 decibels, and can be heard more than a mile away. Cicadas, ditto. The greengrocer cicada, for example, stridulates at 120 decibels, matching the noise level of an airplane engine just before lift-off.

But natural sounds hardly have the same effect on us as their artificial counterparts. In a 2017 study that used brain scans and heart-rate monitors along with behavioural experiments, people showed a high level of stress when exposed to artificial noise. Natural sounds, on the other hand, helped the body relax and function better, while the former exacerbated the body's 'fight or flight' response.

While walking through the desert, I found that the 'noise' of the land does not grate on my nerves the way a car roaring past on baked asphalt at sixty miles an hour does. I wince at the sound of a revving motorbike but revel in the trumpeting of an elephant.

The horn of a truck sets my teeth on edge, but I can listen to an orchestra of *Pompona imperatoria* – the cicadas in the old forests of Borneo which sound just like a truck horn – for hours.

Similarly, studies have found that urban noise – especially those in the lower frequencies – affects birds and how they vocalize. Artificial low-frequency sounds mask how birdsong carries through the air. Some birds, consequently, are forced to increase the amplitude of their songs in order to be heard above the urban buzz. Others sing at night or even change their songs. These changes have been found to depress their chances of finding mates.

I'm on my bed, listening to the sounds of midnight in Bangalore. My neighbour's AC unit turns on, loud in the night's hush, then suddenly falls silent. Through the window behind my headboard I can hear crickets of two kinds: one supplying a constant background chizzzzz, while another plays a two-tone tree-tree, tree-tree. A single frog croaks briefly. A distant barn owl screeches. A street dog barks in the village behind our colony. Then another, and another. The crickets pause, then start up again.

From the window in front of me I see a cloche of stars. A David Wagoner poem sounds gently in my mind:

> When Laurens van der Post one night
> In the Kalihari Desert told the Bushmen
> He couldn't hear the stars
> Singing, they didn't believe him. They looked at him,
> Half-smiling. They examined his face
> To see whether he was joking
> Or deceiving them ...[2]

Over the next hour, the night subsides around me. The crickets stop stridulating. The dogs are not barking anymore. Everywhere there is the silence of the night at rest.

I try to catch the sound of stars singing.

EPILOGUE
Learning to See

What I stand for is what I stand on.

WENDELL BERRY,
Standing by Words[1]

FLYING HIGHER THAN MOUNT EVEREST, I LOOK DOWN FROM THE smudged, double-glassed oval porthole of a commercial plane; 37,000 feet below me I see a twisting, turning blue-and-white river, braiding into itself silt and sand. On its banks are hamlets and a mosaic of green and brown farmland. A bridge straddles the river; clumps of trees punctuate the landscape.

Half an hour later, another river snakes below me. This one is browner, thicker, carrying more water, sand and silt. Big towns sprawl on its banks. Cocooned within our airborne tube and disconnected from the land below, my fellow passengers snooze with the shades pulled down.

I turn to the map on the screen embedded in the seat-back in front of me and trace the flight's path. We are over the Ganga, where it bends into West Bengal from Bihar. Just two days prior, I was in that area. On an almond-shaped wooden fishing boat, we had pushed upriver and gone downstream all week long. The monsoon freshet was abating and the water level was decreasing slowly, revealing old silt islands, birthing new ones.

What I knew from being on the river, that I could never have known from flying high above it, was that it behaved differently on either side of the bend. The left bank was vastly unlike the right bank. The people on either side lived disparate lives, they did not speak the same language, they grew different varieties of crops and rice; they harvested at different times and in vastly dissimilar ways. They experienced the same river differently. And this becomes clear only at ground level, while moving slowly through the landscape and paying close attention.

That process of 'seeing', where we experience a landscape with all our senses, is unavailable to us when we cocoon ourselves in planes and cars and buses and trains, rushing through the terrain without experiencing it. I have learned over time that it is essential to move at a human pace rather than a machine's; to be alive with all our senses in order to begin to truly know. Not unlike the way the shepherds in the deep Thar keenly understand the desert and its rhythms, or how the fishers in the Sundarban are one with the river, unlocking its secrets and deftly negotiating the dangers lurking within its dark waters.

A knowledge of hyperlocal geographies, of the undulations and perturbations of the land over small distances and how these change over seasons, is not only vital to survival but also integral to our resilience in the face of changes in climate. And it is that very intimate, hyperlocal knowledge that is fast eroding today, as traditional livelihoods become unviable in the face of degraded landscapes and people are forced to move away from lands which they know deeply, to desperately find work in cities that are incongruous to their ways.

By some projections, over 200 million people are on the move in South Asia, displaced from their traditional lands, pin-balling from one city to the next. Imagine their progeny, our future generations, growing up with no knowledge of the traditional livelihoods that have sustained their ancestors, nor suited for any meaningful urban employment. We are on the cusp of a humanitarian disaster of colossal proportions.

Nowhere is the value of understanding local geographies more eroded than in our cities. Take the city I live in, for example, a ballooning metropolis housing thirteen million people and counting, and one of the fastest growing cities in the world as measured by increase in influx by the hour. Bangalore sits smack in the centre of peninsular India, perched 900 metres above sea level; it has no perennial rivers or water sources.

In the sixteenth century, a local chieftain named Kempe Gowda and the rulers who followed him built and maintained an ingenious cascading chain of lakes and wetlands so that the excess in one water body would flow through to the next and so on, down the chain. Maps from Bangalore's past indicate that, at one point, the city had over a thousand lakes. Water was plentiful, floods were unknown.

The latter half of the twentieth century ushered in a new buzzword: development. Land for industry and later, big tech, became the most precious commodity; water bodies were 'reclaimed', superimposed with concrete. By the 1960s, there were only 280 lakes left. At the time of writing, there are just eighty, many of which are already facing encroachment; almost all are putrid with sewage and untreated industrial waste, and not one can supply potable water to the population. The cascading chain of lakes designed to drain the land and recharge groundwater has been irreparably broken, built over and choked.

During the heavier-than-normal monsoons of 2022, large parts of Bangalore became submerged. It rained continuously for a couple days in September, and the waters could find nowhere to go. And so it found its own level, flowing downstream, seeking the lowest lands and collecting in the depressions – areas that were once wetlands and overflows from interconnected lake systems and have since been built over.

One particular suburb, a conglomeration of giant tech parks and swanky gated communities, hit the headlines; viral images of the inundated basements of million-dollar residential properties, Jaguars, Bentleys, Audis and Mercedes Benzes floating amidst the detritus circulated on social media. And still the waters rose, seeping into the ground floors, drowning expensive carpets and designer furniture.

The CEOs and leaders of Bangalore's vaunted tech companies had to be evacuated by inflatable boats and hardy tractors. The shanties that had mushroomed around these gated communities to service them were washed away. The waters from just two days of heavy rain took several days to recede; daily life took weeks to return to normalcy, property of all sorts was lost forever.

Woe-is-us postmortems in the aftermath conveniently shifted the blame for the incalculable losses onto that readymade scapegoat: 'climate change'. The government officials who had given indiscriminate building permissions and the builders who had flouted all norms to build over storm water drains looked the other way.

These stories, unfortunately, are not particular to Bangalore or to big cities.

In the freezing winter of 2023, residents of the pilgrimage town of Joshimath in the Himalaya were forced out of their houses when cracks began to appear in the walls, through the foundations, and on the roads. Unchecked tunnelling and drilling, road-cutting and construction have long been the suspects. The region has always been prone to landslides. The town of Joshimath, 2,000 metres above sea level, sits on the remains of an old landslide. But warnings over the years, from geologists and hydrologists have been ignored – here and throughout the Himalayan region. After the cracks appeared at Joshimath, alarm bells were sounded by towns all across the young mountain range.

Cities big and small across South Asia increasingly suffer from all manner of environmental hazards due to ill-conceived development carried out by ivory-tower 'city planners' who have not attempted to understand the topographies of the lands they are remaking in the name of development.

Even so, much of the sub-continent still has its ecological assemblage in some semblance of intactness, giving it a fighting chance to make itself resilient in the face of change. All we need to reclaim even broken cities like Bangalore is a willingness to go back to basics, to understand and acknowledge the local geography, and the inclination to work with the land rather than in defiance of it.

The ideas to effect change, to make our cities water-secure, to make our mountains safe and rivers ecologically healthy, exist. The solutions – sometimes disarmingly simple and not requiring expensive technology – are at hand.

I peep out of the porthole; below me stretches the incredibly biodiverse Western Ghats – a chain of heavily forested hills that runs down the spine of the Indian peninsula's western coast. Somewhere below me is a little piece of land I steward. This piece of forest land on the eastern escarpment of the Ghats, is contiguous on three sides with forests and bordered on the fourth by cultivated fields.

I had long dreamed of stewarding – one never 'owns' the land – a patch and spending years getting to know it well. I have lived all my life in cities; looking after this piece of forest will be an extended learning experience.

Living on – and with – the land brings lessons every day. I lean back in my seat and close my eyes, letting my mind drift to one October morning in 2021. I had woken up to the three-toned hoot of a fish owl that had floated up through the mist hanging heavy over the stream that runs through our land. The Hunter's moon had set. Voices drifted over the paddy fields, where the farming families were preparing for the auspicious day ahead. On that day, they would pray to the land, the trees, the fruits, vegetables, cereals, soil – to everything that sustained them. 'Bhoomi Hunime' – full moon of the land – they call it.

The full moon after the festival of lights, Diwali, traditionally marks the end of the monsoon and heralds winter. But in 2021, the monsoon ignored the calendar and refused to retreat. Doom-black clouds raced in from the southwest and pelted the paddy fields, the trees, banana plantations and the areca palms heavy with ripening fruit. The forecast was for more rain, which spelled bad news for the farmers. The paddy had ripened; some of it had been harvested. Rain falling on the harvested grain caused the paddy to germinate and spoil. In 2021, rice and wheat farmers across peninsular India lost their crops to unseasonable rainfall.

Even as they prepared the festive offerings to honour the land and its gifts, the local farmers were perturbed. In the region known as Malenadu, the land of rain in the south Indian state of Karnataka, October would never be wet and August never dry. The monsoon here was always blindingly heavy but steady and dependable – a much-anticipated renewal and rejuvenation for the parched earth. But by Diwali, in late October or early November, the skies would have long cleared.

No longer. 'These are strange times,' the farmers say. The rains seem to follow no rules. The past year has seen cloudbursts and sudden floods, and then an abrupt ceasing of all precipitation mid-monsoon. It drenches and desiccates, erodes and parches at will, drowning hopes, deepening debts, throwing aeons of agrarian rhythms out of whack.

The old ways are changing too. There is an increasing push towards 'cash crops' – lucrative but water-intensive, thus potentially disastrous in places prone to droughts and in the face of uncertain monsoon patterns. The time-tested, resilient ways of life that were built on a deep understanding of one's environs, is dying out.

But I don't despair – not yet. There are those all over the Indian subcontinent who have immersed themselves in landscapes and show us the way. The Chhattar Singhs who are one with their desertlands, the Katons who can negotiate every rock and shrub in the mountains, the Lekhus who can read rivers and summon dolphins, the Wangchuks who use the local topography to preserve their world in the face of humongous odds, and millions of others who live attentively so they may still be able to hear the land, understand it, show it respect, adapt and survive.

In my nascent journey, in sharing time with such people in their milieu, seeing through their eyes and contrasting their vision with the land-gaze of interlopers, I have come to agree with a wise writer's words:

'The hardest thing of all to see is what is really there.'

GLOSSARY OF LOCAL WORDS

Pronunciation Guide: Capitalized letters denote harder sounds; lowercase letters denote softer sounds. Double letters denote a stress on the sound. Where the L and the N are capitalized, the tongue should hit the roof of the mouth – sounds not in English, but used in many Indian languages.

-sar	-suhr	suffix to denote a water body – a pond or a lake
aagor	aagOHr	a scree catchment
aak		*Calotropis gigantea*
baata	baaTa	a dish prepared with the buds of the lana plant
baaval		petrichor
bajra	baajrAH	pearl millet
bantal	bun-tal	a relaxed conversation
bawliya		*Prosopis juliflora*, an invasive tree in India
beri	bAYri	a percolation well
bhey		a natural rock formation of a stone cistern
bhikari		beggar, in Hindi
Bhil	bheel	a tribe in India

bhulan		*Platanista gangetica minor*, Indus river dolphin
bigha		a measure of land area varying locally from 1/3 to 1 acre (1/8 to 2/5 hectare)
bordi		Ziziphus species of tree; Indian jujube
cha		tea, in Bengali
chaadar	chaadurr	overflow from the khadeen
chapori		silt island, in Assamese
char		silt island, in Bengali
chhand	cHHannd	a rhyme sung as a chant
chhinto	cHHinTo	sprinkles of rain
chinkara		*Gazella bennettii*, antelope
dhaani	DhaaNi	a shepherding outpost usually consisting of a lean-to
dharolyuo	dhaaroLyoo	a veil of cloud seen bridging the sky and earth
dhora	dhOHraH	bund
dhundh		clouds slightly heavier than paans
diara		silt island, in Bihar
eyloor	eyyloor	cirrus clouds
garam	garam	warm; in this case (of meat) meaning high-calorific
geru	gAYroo	red oxide
gharial		*Gavialis gangeticus*, a fish-eating crocodile with a long snout that ends in a bulge that looks like a *ghada*, meaning pot in Hindi
ghataatope	ghaTaaTope	many kanthi clouds

ghutyo	ghuTyo	an asphyxiating feeling due to high humidity and heat
giddh		vulture
godawn	go-daawan	*Ardeotis nigriceps*, great Indian bustard
golpata	gol-paata	*Nypa fruticans*, nipa palm
hilsa		*Tenualosa ilisha*, an Indian shad
ilish		*Tenualosa ilisha*, the hilsa fish, in Bengali
jaal	jaal	*Salvadora oleoides*
jama	jaamaa	long coat
janeu	janeoh	a sacred thread worn by Brahmins
jutti	juttee	handmade leather slides with an upwardly curved pointed tip; often embroided with cotton, gold or silver thread
kair	kAYr	*Capparis decidua*, a spindly desert tree with caper-like fruit consumed fresh and dried
kalaan	kaLaan	heavy rainclouds coming in from the northwest
kamarband	kummerbundh	waistband
kambavala/ karamadi		shore-seine fishing, in Malayalam
kanthi	kaa(n)Thi	cumulus clouds on the horizon
khadeen	kha-Deen	a water-harvesting structure, a rain-fed field and food bowl all rolled into one
khal	khaal	channel of water, in Bengali
khanjar	khanjar	short, curved dagger
khann		mine, in Hindi

kharif	khareef	autumn crop sown during the rains
khatiya		wooden cot with a cotton cross-weave
khejri	khej-Di	*Prosopis cineraria*, a holy tree in the desert, the long fruit pods of which are consumed fresh and dried as 'sangri'
khera	kheDa	small village
khod		thatch
kohra	k-OH-raa	dense fog, in Hindi
kolohi/kalash		curved pot topped with betel leaves and a coconut, meant to symbolize abundance
kuan	kuaa(n) (a nasal hint)	well
laal saa		red tea; the 'ch' of 'cha' or tea is pronounced 'sa' in certain Bangladeshi dialects of Bengali
lana	laaNaa	Haloxylon species of plant
lashipa	la-shee-pah	working for the joy of it
maachh		fish, in Bengali
maali		gardener
magra		scree
maund	mawndh	an Indian unit of weight equivalent to about 37 kilograms
Mising/ Mishing/Miri		a tribe in Assam and Arunachal Pradesh
mojri	mojDi	locally handmade leather slip-ons with curved, upturned, pointed front (jutti)
moulvi		Muslim doctor of law

nahar		canal, in Hindi
nodi	nodhi	river, in Bengali
oran		sacred grove, in Marwari
paans	paa(n)s	consolidated teetar pankhi clouds forming a light uneven blanket
palar pani	paa-lar paani	surface water of lakes, ponds, rivers
pani hari		water carriers: women with pots on their heads
pankh	pa(n)kh	wings
patali kuan	pataaLi kuaa(n) (a nasal hint)	a thick, dense, round flatbread made of millet flour
phog		*Calligonum polygonoides*
pilu	peeloo	*Salvadora persica*
punya	pooNya	good karma
rabi	rabee	crop sown after the rains and reaped in spring
raksha bandhan		a custom where a sister ties a band around the brother's wrist and he pledges to protect her; celebrated annually in India
rejwani pani	rAYjwani paani	water contained in the aquifer that sits above the gypsum layer running through the deep desert
rota	rOH-Ta	a thick, dense, round flatbread made of millet flour
saafa		turban
saahas		courage
sangri	saangri	long pods of the khejri tree which forms a staple diet of Rajasthanis
sarkanda		Saccharum species of tall grass

sevan		*Lasirius scindicus*, a local nutritious grass
shushuk		*Platanista gangetica*, Gangetic river dolphin
taka	Taakaa	money, in Bengali
teetar	teetarr	partridge
teetar-pankhi	teetar pa(n)khee	cirrocumulus clouds, resembling the pattern on a partridge's wings
teli		oil seller
ubrelyo		spent clouds
vaazh	vaaZH (ZH = a sound between a harsh L sound that hits the roof of the mouth and a D)	the high watermark of rainwater that rolls down the aagor and comes to stop at the bund
zamindaar		landowner, in Hindi

NOTES

1. Katherine Boo, *Behind the Beautiful Forevers: Life, Death and Hope in a Mumbai Undercity* (New York: Random House, 2012).

PROLOGUE: GATHERING STRING

1. Wendell Berry, *Standing by Words: Essays*, (Berkeley: Counterpoint, 2011).
2. Sálim Ali, *The Book of Indian Birds* (Bombay: Bombay Natural History Society, 1996).
3. An excerpt from Wendell Berry, *Reverdure* (Colorado: The Press at Colorado College, 1974).
4. Rainer Maria Rilke, *Letters to a Young Poet* (New York: Dover Publications, 2021).
5. Rob Nixon, *Slow Violence and the Environmentalism of the Poor* (Cambridge: Harvard University Press, 2011).

PART I: THE DESERT

A Liquid Memory

1. A. Mishra, *The Radiant Raindrops of Rajasthan* (New Delhi: Research Foundation for Science, Technology and Ecology, 2001).

The Landscape of Loss

1. Barry Lopez, *About this Life: Journeys on the Threshold of Memory* (New York: Penguin Random House, 1998).

2. desert antelopes
3. S. Nadeem Ali Rezavi, 'Kuldhara in Jaisalmer State–Social and Economic Implications of the Remains of a Medieval Settlement', *Proceedings of the Indian History Congress* 56 (1995), 312–32.
4. Martin von Mirbach, 'Inside and Out [Review of *About This Life: Journeys on the Threshold of Memory* by Barry Lopez]', *Alternatives Journal* 25, no. 2 (1999): 37–38. http://www.jstor.org/stable/45032111.
5. Chhattar Singh points to a dead vulture in the distance.

PART 2: VEINS OF OUR LAND

In the Shifting Embrace of the Ganga

1. Greater adjutant, Wikipedia.
2. G. T. Braulik, F. I. Archer, Uzma Khan, et al. 'Taxonomic revision of the South Asian River dolphins (Platanista): Indus and Ganges River dolphins are separate species'. *Mar Mam Sci.* 2021. 37: 1022–1059.
3. Gharials, Wikipedia.
4. Sudipta Sen, *Ganges: The Many Pasts of an Indian River*, (United Kingdom: Yale University Press, 2019).
5. Graham Chapman & Kalyan Rudra, 'Water as Foe, Water as Friend'. *Journal of South Asian Development*, 2007. 2: 19-49.
6. Abul Fazl-i-allami, *Ain-i-akbari, vol 2* (Calcutta: Royal Asiatic Society Of Bengal, 1949)
7. Graham Chapman & Kalyan Rudra, 'Water as Foe, Water as Friend'. *Journal of South Asian Development*, 2007. 2: 19-49.
8. R. H. Colebrooke, 'On the Course of the Ganges, through Bengal'. *Asiatick Researches*. 1803; 7: 1–31.
9. Kalyan Rudra, 'Shifting of the Ganga and Land Erosion in West Bengal: A Socio-Ecological Viewpoint', *Centre for Development and Environmental Policy Occasional Paper 8*. 2006.
10. T. K. Das, S. K. Haldar, I. D. Gupta, & Sayanti Sen, 'River Bank Erosion Induced Human Displacement and Its Consequences'. *Living Reviews in Landscape Research*. 2014. 8: 5–35.
11. Ganges, Wikipedia.
12. Polina Lemenkova. 'Sediment thickness in the Bay of Bengal and

Andaman Sea compared with topography and geophysical settings by GMT'. *Ovidius University Annals Series: Civil Engineering.* 2020. 22: 13-22.

13. Sudipta Sen, *Ganges: The Many Pasts of an Indian River*, (United Kingdom: Yale University Press, 2019).
14. Muhammad Ibn-'Abdallāh Ibn-Battūta. *The Travels of Ibn Battuta: in the Near East, Asia and Africa, 1325-1354.* (London: Dover Publications, 2004).
15. Kalyan Rudra, 'Shifting of the Ganga and Land Erosion in West Bengal: A Socio-Ecological Viewpoint', *Centre for Development and Environmental Policy Occasional Paper 8*. 2006.
16. Ibid.
17. Sudipto Mitra, 'Nationalising Ruins: Contested Identities of the Ruins of Gour and Pandua'. *Presidency Historical Review*, 2016. pp 55–82.
18. Sudipta Sen, 'Of Holy Rivers and Human Rights: Protecting the Ganges by Law'. Yale University Press. Online. https://yalebooks.yale.edu/2019/04/25/of-holy-rivers-and-human-rights-protecting-the-ganges-by-law/#:~:text=By%20ruling%20that%20polluting%20the,health%20and%20well%2Dbeing%E2%80%9D.

A Fleeting Flash of Fin

1. Muhammad Ibn-'Abdallāh Ibn-Battūta, *The Travels of Ibn Battuta* (London: John Murray, 1829).
2. Kalyan Rudra, 'Shifting of the Ganga and Land Erosion in West Bengal: A Socio-Ecological Viewpoint', *Centre for Development and Environmental Policy Occasional Paper* 8 (2006), 8.
3. Ibid.
4. Aman Sood, 'Beas reserve going dry, aquatic life in danger', *Tribune*, 30 March 2018. Available at: https://www.tribuneindia.com/news/archive/punjab/beas-reserve-going-dry-aquatic-life-in-danger-566450.
5. *Lipotes vedillifer*

Fading to Black

1. 'The Assam Earthquake – 15 August 1950', *Koi-hai,* 16 October 2006. Available at: http://www.koi-hai.com/Default.aspx?id=490706#Assam Earthquake1950.
2. Kalyan Rudra, 'Shifting of the Ganga and Land Erosion in West Bengal: A Socio-Ecological Viewpoint', *Centre for Development and Environmental Policy Occasional Paper* 8 (2006), 8.
3. 'Harike Wetland.' Wikipedia. Wikimedia Foundation, 27 December 2022. Available at: https://en.wikipedia.org/wiki/Harike_Wetland.
4. James Coley, *Journal of the Sutlej Campaign of 1845–6 And also of Lord Hardinge's Tour in the Following Winter*, available on Internet Archive.
5. Sood, 'Beas reserve going dry, aquatic life in danger'.
6. Madan Kumar, 'CM opposes more barrages in Ganga', *Times of India*, 13 April 2015. Available at: http://timesofindia.indiatimes.com/articleshow/46899750.cms?utm_source=contentofinterest&utm_medium=text&utm_campaign=cppst.
7. Nachiket Kelkar, 'A summary analysis of the ecological impacts of the National Waterways Bill (2015)', *SANDRP*, 19 February 2016. Available at: https://sandrp.in/2016/02/19/digging-our-rivers-graves/.

PART 3: AN ERODING MARGIN

On the Brink of Brine

1. Nachiket Kelkar, 'A summary analysis of the ecological impacts of the National Waterways Bill (2015)'.
2. Aldo Leopold, *A Sand County Almanac: And Sketches Here and There* (Oxford and New York: Oxford University Press, 2020).
3. Francis Kingdon-Ward, 'The Assam Earthquake of 1950', *The Geographical Journal* 119, 2 (1953), 169–82.
4. 'The Assam Earthquake – August 15th 1950', *Koi-hai.*
5. Ibid.

Jewels by the Sea

1. As Rachel Carson notes in her excellent book *The Edge of the Sea.*
2. Also see *Marine Life of Mumbai*, for example.

Eating Up the Coast

1. Walter Scott, *The Antiquary* (Edinburgh: James Ballantine & Co., 1816).
2. Sunil Amrith, *Crossing the Bay of Bengal* (Cambridge: Harvard University Press, 2013).
3. Samanth Subramanian, *Following Fish: One Man's Journey into the Food and Culture of the Indian Coast* (New York: St Martin's Press, 2016).
4. 'Valiyathura housing project hanging fire', *New Indian Express*, 16 October 2020. Available at: https://www.newindianexpress.com/cities/thiruvananthapuram/2020/oct/16/valiyathura-housing-project-hanging-fire-2210733.html.

PART 4: THE THIRD POLE

When the Glaciers Disappear

1. Johann Gottlob Schneider, *Aristotle's History of Animals: In Ten Books* (London: G. Bell, 1878).

A Coup on the Roof of the World

1. Sudarshan Rodriguez, Devi Subramanian, Aarthi Sridhar, Manju Menon, and Kartik Shanker, 'Policy Brief: Seawalls', *UNDP/UNTRS*, Chennai and ATREE, Bangalore, India 8 (2008).

Into the Hidden Land

1. It pushes east for almost 1,625 kilometres, then makes a hairpin bend and vanishes into a deep gorge that straddles the border between China's Tibet Autonomous Region (TAR) and India.

PART 5: THE SOUND OF CITIES

Where the Wild Things Still Are

1. Justice William O. Douglas remarks at a conference sponsored by the American Histadrut Cultural Exchange Institute, Harriman, New York, 17–19 February 1967. *Government and the Democratic Process: A Symposium by American and Israeli Experts*, Judd L. Teller ed., 1969, 16.
2. John Renard ed., *Tales of God's Friends: Islamic Hagiography in Translation* (Berkeley: University of California Press, 2009).
3. Willem van Schendel, *A History of Bangladesh* (Cambridge: Cambridge University Press, 2009).

Listening to Landscapes

1. An excerpt from 'Thirteen Ways of Looking at a Blackbird. Available at: https://www.poetryfoundation.org/poems/45236/thirteen-ways-of-looking-at-a-blackbird.
2. An excerpt from 'The Silence of the Stars'. Available at: https://www.poemhunter.com/poem/the-silence-of-the-stars/.

EPILOGUE: LEARNING TO SEE

1. Wendell Berry, *What I Stand On: The Collected Essays of Wendell Berry 1969–2017* (New York: Library of America, 2019).

GRATITUDE

Firstly, I am indebted to a chance meeting with Gautam John, the ball he set rolling, and the interest Rohini Nilekani showed in my work. This book would not have been possible without your support. Thank you, Rohini Nilekani Philanthropies, for believing in and standing by me.

Once in a lifetime, if you are lucky, you meet someone who becomes mentor, guide, sounding board, travel partner, lodestar, a willing butt of jokes, sparring partner and the closest of friends. I got twice lucky. Thank you, Prem Panicker and Paul Salopek, for way more than you can ever imagine and I can ever put into words. I am what I am in large part due to all that I continue to learn from you both.

And Prem? I know you will cringe, but I have to say this: how lucky I am to have 'possibly the best editor in the whole wide world' (Don Belt's words – and he would know) in my corner. 'Thank you' does not begin to describe how grateful I am to that Twitter exchange in early 2012. You've always been a … boulder, my friend!

I stand on the shoulders of giants. These are people with humongous hearts, generous with time and hospitality, unfailing in their attention and magnanimous with their knowledge. To you, I am indebted for life, for what you have given I will forever carry with me: Chhattar Singh, Pradip Krishen, Harsha J., Payal Mehta, Manori Gunawardena, Pubudhu, Aparajita Dutta, Divya Mudappa, T. R. Shankar Raman, Pradip Chatterjee, Milan Das, Himanshu Thakkar, Sanjoy Hazarika, Arupjyoti Saikia, Chandan Mahanta, Radha Rangarajan, Raji Sunderkrishnan, the late Dr Latha Anantha, Nilanjana Roy, Ravindra Nath, Lakhi Hazarika, Shilppika Bordoloi, Farhad Contractor, Sonam Wangchuk, Mingyur Gya, Tarikul Islam, Kalyan Rudra, Shahryar Caesar Rahman, Pia and Mithva Krishen, Nachiket Kelkar, Jagdish Krishnaswamy, Subhasis Dey, Oken Tayeng, Katon Moyong, Dr Hema Somanathan, Dr V. V. Belavadi, S. Dilip Roy, S. Vishwanath, Mame Khan, Joydeep Gupta and the Third Pole, Kuntal Kapadia, Gayatri Vaswani, Abi T. Vanak, Chandrima Das, Saloni Bhatia, Rob Kunzig and many more. I keep an updated list here: aratikumarrao.com/gratitude

My family – Sanjana and Sanat – I argue with you and fight you, but I love you far more, and will never lose sight of the fact that your trust in me as I wander is what keeps me going. Amma, Mamma, Papa, Supi – to you I owe an immense debt for all that you have taught me. Anjilina, Ranjita, Srinivas, Anita, Raghu, Chandri: without you, I cannot do what I do. Thank you. Shyn, Shadow, Zorro – your presence is pure balm.

Mita Kapur, thank you for your support. And thank you, Teesta Guha Sarkar, for coming to me with the idea for this book. I had not dared imagine it, and you made it real.

My deepest gratitude to the people I have met on this journey. You trusted me with your lived experiences, welcomed me into your homes, shared your meals with me, gave me rides, translated for me and taught me about worlds within your worlds. You continue to keep me honest, and continually remind me how to truly 'see'.

And finally, thank you, dear reader, for your time, interest and attention.

ABOUT THE AUTHOR

Arati Kumar-Rao is an environmental photographer, writer, artist and National Geographic Explorer documenting the effects of environmental degradation. Working primarily in the Indian subcontinent, she chronicles anthropogenic changes in landscapes and their fallouts on livelihood, culture and biodiversity. She communicates through still and moving images, soundscapes, longform narratives and art. Her work has appeared in *National Geographic Magazine*, *Hindu*, *Guardian*, *Hindustan Times*, *Mint* and BBC Outside Source, among other outlets. She was named in the BBC 100 Women list of 2023.

When not on assignment, she divides her time between the Western Ghats and Bangalore, where she is a happy mother to three rescued indoor cats.